Better Homes and Gardens®

CROSS-STITCH SAMPLERS

First Edition. Ninth Printing, 1991.
Library of Congress Catalog Card Number: 85-73115
ISBN: 0-696-01510-2 (hard cover)
ISBN: 0-696-01512-9 (trade paperback)

BETTER HOMES AND GARDENS® BOOKS

Editor: Gerald M. Knox
Art Director: Ernest Shelton
Managing Editor: David A. Kirchner
Copy and Production Editors: James D. Blume,
    Marsha Jahns, Rosanne Weber Mattson,
    Mary Helen Schiltz

Crafts Editor: Jean LemMon
Senior Crafts Books Editor: Joan Cravens
Associate Crafts Books Editor: Sara Jane Treinen
    Judith Veeder

Associate Art Directors: Linda Ford Vermie,
    Neoma Alt West, Randall Yontz
Assistant Art Directors: Lynda Haupert,
    Harijs Priekulis, Tom Wegner
Senior Graphic Designers: Jack Murphy, Stan Sams,
    Darla Whipple-Frain
Graphic Designers: Mike Burns, Sally Cooper,
    Blake Welch, Brian Wignall, Kimberly Zarley

Vice President, Editorial Director: Doris Eby
Executive Director, Editorial Services: Duane L. Gregg

President, Book Group: Fred Stines
Director of Publishing: Robert B. Nelson
Vice President, Retail Marketing: Jamie Martin
Vice President, Direct Marketing: Arthur Heydendael

CROSS–STITCH SAMPLERS
Crafts Editor: Sara Jane Treinen
Contributing Editor: Laura Holtorf Collins
Copy and Production Editor: Marsha Jahns
Graphic Designer: Darla Whipple-Frain
Electronic Text Processor: Donna Russell

Cover project: See page 36.

CONTENTS

CELEBRATIONS
OF
HOME

TO STITCH
WITH PRIDE

Few needlecraft traditions are as enduring—and endearing—as samplers. By stitching a sampler, whether it's an album of favorite motifs or a decorative design for your home, you are creating not only something beautiful for yourself or your loved ones but your own niche in our needlework heritage as well.

In this chapter are handsome pictures and other projects for you to stitch in honor of home and family. Wherever you live—in the city, in the suburbs, or out in the country—you're sure to find a design that suits your personal style *and* your sentiments exactly.

The cross-stitch sampler, *right,* combines a popular saying and a verse often found in old needlework books. These typical sampler phrases are topped by a charming scene and surrounded with a delicate geometric border. Stitched on hardanger cloth using six-strand embroidery floss, the picture measures 15½x20 inches. The chart for the design appears on pages 14 and 15. Instructions begin on page 16.

Be it ever so humble
there's no place like
Home

With Fingers so nimble, she plied her needle and thimble
Nancy Helgeson, her work 1986

"Heartfelt" certainly describes the sentiment conveyed in these samplers—both because of the charming scenes found on each one and because hearts (a traditional sampler motif) are incorporated so gracefully into the designs.

Reminiscent of folk art renditions of rural life, the cheerful farm scene, *opposite,* is stitched using No. 5 pearl cotton thread on hardanger cloth.

The sampler features simple drawings of a farmhouse and family, fruit trees that suggest an orchard, and farm animals familiar even to city folk. Fanciful flowers, birds, and butterflies enhance the border on this 22½x25-inch design. Directions begin on page 21.

Stitched on 18-count even-weave fabric using embroidery floss, the 17¼x18-inch picture, *above,* is proof of the vitality of time-honored techniques and designs in sampler stitchery. For example, eighteenth-century needlecrafters added scenes to their samplers to complement the alphabets and borders of earlier days. Buildings, animals, trees, and human figures became popular stitchery motifs—and remain so even today.

Eighteenth-century stitchers also framed their scenes with borders worked partly or entirely around them. The borders often were based on wavy lines, with motifs such as hearts, tucked into the curves.

How-to instructions for this sampler begin on page 23.

Samplers aren't just pretty pictures to hang on the wall. In the sixteenth and seventeenth centuries—when paper was scarce and expensive—samplers were probably notebooks on fabric, much like the sketchbooks of today's cross-stitchers.

Needlecrafters in those days stitched their samplers to keep track of patterns for alphabets, numbers, and pretty motifs that they could use to embellish and identify their clothing and household items. Perhaps they referred to their samplers in the same way that modern-day stitchers refer to their charts, choosing from among the designs to stitch the ones they love best.

Like many antique samplers, the design framed in the tilt-top table, *opposite,* features letters and numerals, floral and geometric bands and motifs, and a favorite saying. Stitch this 9½x15-inch design (before framing) on black 14-count Aida cloth, using embroidery floss. Then set it into an oval frame and display it with pride. (The source for the frame, *opposite,* and the table, *above,* is noted in the instructions.)

Or, use the oval sampler as a pattern guide for another project. To make the 9x9-inch table insert, *above,* stitch some of the bands from the oval design into borders surrounding a monogram created with initials shown on the sampler. Directions for the oval design are on page 23. Instructions for the table insert begin on page 26.

The blue and white sampler, *right,* like all antique samplers, is a pattern book of elegant motifs that you can adapt to a host of home furnishings accents, such as the footstool, *above.*

Stitch the 26 designs in the sampler using two shades of blue cotton embroidery floss (or colors of your choice) on 14-count white Aida cloth to make the 15½x19½-inch picture shown. Then repeat the designs on other projects, changing the background fabrics, colors, and sizes of the motifs as you desire.

The 12-inch-square footstool, for example, also is cross-stitched using floss, but the stitches are worked over 10-count waste canvas onto white, dress-weight wool. (See page 78 for tips on using waste canvas.)

You also might use the geometric borders, alone or in combination, as embellishments for bed, bath, and table linens. Stitch them in two shades of one color, as shown here, or in an assortment of your favorite tints.

If you vary the colors, however, you might want to begin by charting the designs on graph paper using colored pencils or markers.

Charting with pencils or markers will enable you to check your color scheme, *and* it will provide you with an easy-to-follow chart designed just for the project you have in mind.

For instructions for both projects, see pages 18 and 19.

There's no nicer way to have your cross-stitch project always underfoot than with this charming embroidered rug.

Adapted from the sampler alphabet featured on the preceding page, the rug is another example of the versatility of sampler designs. For a similar rug, cross-stitch on 4-mesh-to-the-inch penelope canvas, using ¾-inch-wide strips of ecru polished cotton and nine printed fabrics. The finished design measures 42½x62½ inches. Instructions begin on page 26.

For variety in your sampler stitching, you might try crafting with yarn instead of floss or pearl cotton. The picture shown here, for example, is worked with three-ply crewel wool yarns in vivid colors. Eighteen-count cotton Davosa cloth provides a homespun background for this 18½x25¼-inch design. Instructions are on page 27.

As with the other sampler motifs shown throughout this book, the alphabet, pictorial motifs, and border patterns in this design can be used to embellish and personalize an enormous number of gifts for your home, family, and friends.

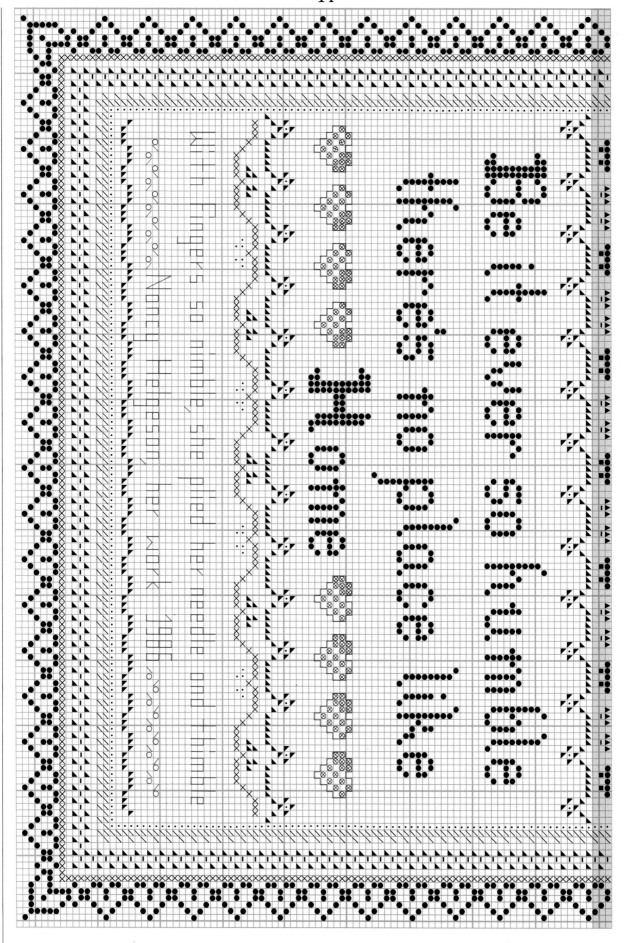

COLOR KEY

815 ● Berry	433 ⊠ Brown	920 ⊟ Light Brown	676 · Yellow
300 ■ Dark Brown	319 ◢ Forest Green	703 ◿ Light Green	519 ◥ Light Blue

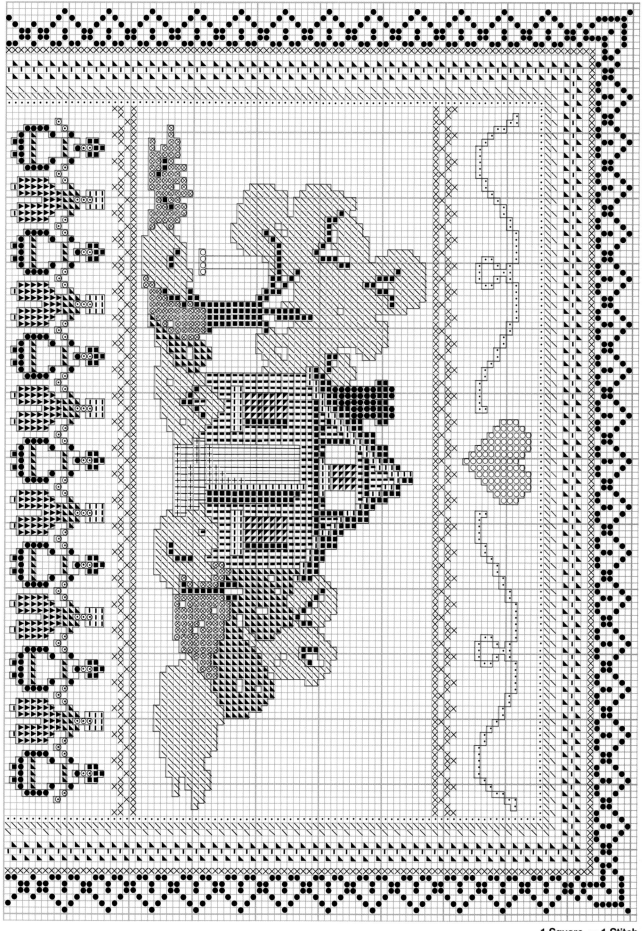

1 Square = 1 Stitch

349 ⊙ Red   310 ▲ Black   738 ▯ Tan   317 ⊞ Dark Gray
700 ⊗ Kelly Green   945 ⊙ Flesh   318 ▯ Light Gray   ☐ White

"Be It Ever So Humble" Sampler

Shown on pages 4–5.

Finished size, framed, is 15½x20 inches.

MATERIALS
18½x23-inch piece of white hardanger
DMC embroidery floss: 3 skeins of berry (815); 2 skeins *each* of dark brown (300), brown (433), and black (310); 1 skein *each* of blue (519), light gray (318), dark gray (317), light brown (920), red (349), flesh (945), yellow (676), light green (703), kelly green (700), forest green (319), and tan (738)
Tapestry needle

INSTRUCTIONS
Before beginning, see the general information on pages 78 and 79 for special cross-stitch tips and techniques, and for materials necessary for working all counted cross-stitch projects.

Refer to the cross-stitch design on pages 14 and 15 and chart your name and year in place on the pattern, using the letters on the pattern as a guide. For best results, chart your name onto graph paper and establish the number of stitches required; then eliminate or add pattern repeats to the existing pattern to accommodate your name.

Measure 3 inches down and 3 inches in from the upper left corner of the fabric; begin stitching there.

Work each cross-stitch over two threads of the fabric. Stitch the borders first and then proceed to fill in the center of the sampler.

With black, work the half-cross-stitches on both sides of your name, backstitch all shapes to outline them, and the saying in the lower portion of the sampler. With green, work backstitches to outline green hearts.

Frame as desired.

Top Left

COLOR KEY
796 ⊠ **Dark Blue**
799 ⧄ **Light Blue**

Bottom Left

1 Square = 1 Stitch

Blue and White Sampler and Footstool

Shown on pages 10–11.

Finished size of framed sampler is 15½x19½ inches. Footstool is 12 inches square.

MATERIALS
For the sampler
22x26-inch piece of 14-count white Aida cloth
DMC embroidery floss: 5 skeins of dark blue (796) and 4 skeins of light blue (799)
Tapestry needle

For the footstool
14-inch square of white wool
DMC embroidery floss: 1 skein *each* of dark blue (796) and light blue (799)
12-inch square of 10-count waste canvas
Footstool with a 9½-inch-square inset (available at crafts shops or by writing to Plain 'n' Fancy, Inc., Box 357, Mathews, VA 23109)

INSTRUCTIONS
For the sampler
Before beginning, see the general information on pages 78 and 79 for special cross-stitch tips and techniques, and for materials necessary for working all counted cross-stitch projects.

Referring to charts, pages 16–19, use two strands of floss to work cross-stitches over one square of the cloth. The shaded portions of the charts on pages 18 and 19 represent stitches already completed from the previous charts (pages 16 and 17) and are indicated for ease in placement of stitches when following from one chart to the next. Do not work the shaded areas.

Measure 4½ inches down and 4½ inches in from the upper left corner of the fabric; begin stitching there. When the stitching is complete, frame as desired.

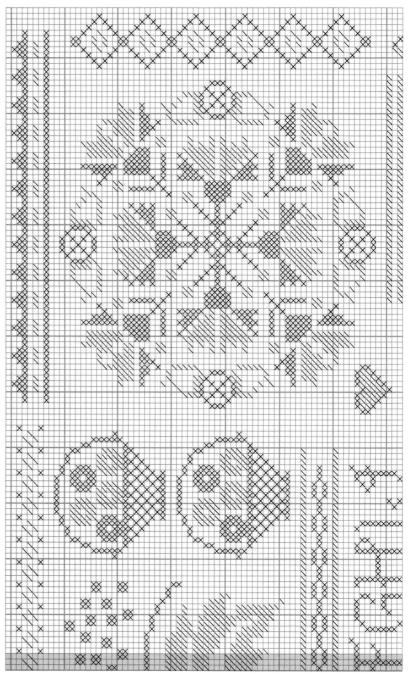

Top Right

For the footstool
Use the motif in the upper right-hand corner of the sampler, page 18. Center and baste the waste canvas to the wool fabric.

Locate the center of both the motif and the fabric and begin stitching there. Use two strands of floss to work the cross-stitches over one space of the canvas.

Complete the motif; then begin to work the border in the eighth thread from the three outside dark blue stitches of the motif. Select a border pattern from the sampler design and adapt the pattern to work the corners and fit the footstool. (The footstool shown uses the border on the top right corner of the sampler.)

Bottom Right

1 Square = 1 Stitch

To remove the waste canvas, dampen the canvas; pull out the horizontal threads, one at a time, and then repeat for the vertical threads.

Center and stretch the finished piece atop footstool insert; staple in place. Finish footstool base as desired. Then mount the insert to the footstool.

COLOR KEY
796 ⊠ Dark Blue
799 ⊡ Light Blue

Bless Our Farm Sampler

"Bless Our Farm" Sampler

Shown on page 6.

Finished size, framed, is 22½x25 inches.

MATERIALS
27x29-inch piece of white hardanger
DMC pearl cotton, Size 5, in the following amounts: 3 skeins of light green (702); 2 skeins *each* of yellow (726), dark orange (351), red (349), dark green (319), and blue (517); and 1 skein *each* of light orange (353), camel (435), brown (400), dark gray (413), and white
Tapestry needle

INSTRUCTIONS
Before beginning, see the general information on pages 78 and 79 for special cross-stitch tips and techniques, and for materials necessary for working all counted cross-stitch projects.

Referring to the chart, *opposite*, locate the center of the design and the center of the fabric; begin stitching there. Use one strand of pearl cotton to work cross-stitches over three threads of fabric.

Stitch butterfly antennae with backstitches over three threads of fabric using dark gray.

Stitch stems of apples and pears with a single backstitch using dark green.

Stitch outlines of sheep and rabbit with backstitches using dark gray; outline white areas only of cow with backstitches using camel.

Chart and work *your* initials and date in the area inside the blue rectangle.

When stitching is complete, frame as desired.

COLOR KEY
400	Brown	702	Light Green
319	Dark Green	353	Light Orange
349	Red	726	Yellow
351	Dark Orange	413	Dark Gray
517	Blue		White
435	Camel		

1 Square = 1 Stitch

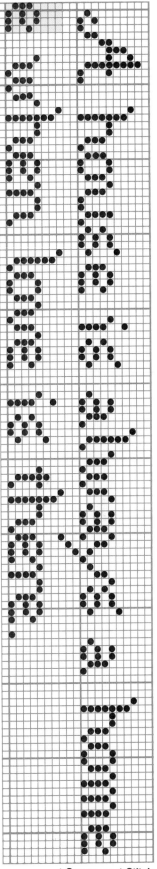

1 Square = 1 Stitch
(over 1 thread of fabric)

CELEBRATIONS OF HOME

"A House Is Always A Home" Sampler

Shown on page 7.

Finished size, framed, is 17¼x18 inches.

MATERIALS
23-inch-square piece of 18-count even-weave fabric
DMC embroidery floss, 1 skein *each* of yellow (743), red (349), dark brown (801), light brown (301), gray (452), light blue (932), dark blue (930), peach (352), green (501), and white
Tapestry needle

INSTRUCTIONS
Before beginning, see the general information on pages 78 and 79 for special cross-stitch tips and techniques, and for materials necessary for working all counted cross-stitch projects.

Chart your name, place, and date on the "stitched by" portion of the pattern, *opposite,* using the letters on the diagram (see page 21) as a guide.

Measure 3 inches down and 3 inches in from the upper left corner of the fabric and begin stitching there.

Use three strands of floss to work the cross-stitches over two threads of the fabric for working the main portions of the sampler as shown on the chart, *opposite.*

Use two strands of floss for working the cross-stitches over

one thread of the fabric for the two written lines (the stitcher's name line and the saying line). See the chart on page 21 for ease in working the saying. *Note:* The shaded portion of this chart is for placement of the following letter (w) only. Do not stitch the shaded portion.

Work the outlines of squirrels, rabbits, and house steps with backstitches over two threads of the fabric with two strands of dark brown floss.

When the stitching is complete, frame as desired.

"Bless This House" Tilt-top Table

Shown on page 8.

Finished size of stitchery, unframed, is 9½x15 inches.

MATERIALS
15½x21-inch piece of 14-count black Aida cloth
DMC embroidery floss: Dark violet (208), light violet (210), light blue (747), blue (807), peach (353), yellow (741), dark pink (891), light pink (894), light green (564), and dark green (992)
Purchased tilt-top table (available through crafts shops or write to Plain 'n' Fancy, Inc., Box 357, Mathews, VA 23109) or oval frame
Tapestry needle

INSTRUCTIONS
Before beginning, see the general information on pages 78 and 79 for special cross-stitch tips and techniques, and for materials necessary for working all counted cross-stitch projects.

Referring to the chart on pages 24 and 25, locate the center of the pattern and the center of the fabric; begin stitching there.

Use two strands of floss to work each cross-stitch over one square of the Aida cloth.

When the stitching is complete, press and frame in the purchased table top or an oval frame.

COLOR KEY
801 ◉ Dark Brown
501 ▲ Green
349 ◪ Red
930 ◼ Dark Blue
301 ⊠ Light Brown
452 ⊞ Gray
932 ⧄ Light Blue
352 Ⅱ Peach
743 ⊟ Yellow
⊙ White

1 Square = 1 Stitch

CELEBRATIONS OF HOME

Fire Screen

COLOR KEY

992	Dark Green	208	Dark Violet	210	Light Violet	747	Light Blue
891	Dark Pink	564	Light Green	741	Yellow	353	Peach
894	Light Pink	564	Half Cross	807	Blue		

1 Square = 1 Stitch

Tabletop Insert Sampler

Shown on page 9.

Finished size of stitchery is 9x9 inches.

MATERIALS
15x15-inch square of white hardanger
DMC embroidery floss: Light green (772), dark green (987), peach (352), dark coral (349), blue (807), bright yellow (741), and violet (208)
Table (available through local crafts shops or write to: Plain 'n' Fancy, Inc., Box 357, Mathews, VA 23109)
Tapestry needle

INSTRUCTIONS
Before beginning, see the general information on pages 78 and 79 for special cross-stitch tips and techniques, and for materials necessary for working all counted cross-stitch projects.

Referring to the pattern, *below,* chart design onto graph paper using felt-tip markers; flop pattern to complete one half of the design. Then chart the mirror image of the existing drawn design to complete the design in all four quadrants. Refer to the top alphabet pattern from the sampler on page 25 to chart initials in the center of the design.

Measure 3 inches down and 3 inches in from the upper left corner of the fabric; mark this point with a water-soluble pen. Begin stitching at this point.

Use two strands of floss to work each cross-stitch over two threads of the hardanger.

When the sampler is complete, press and staple it to the tabletop insert or frame as desired. Mount the insert to the table following the manufacturer's directions.

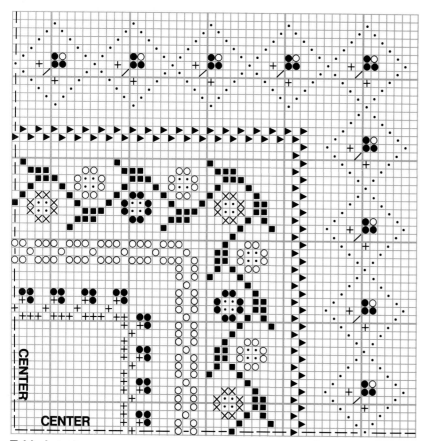

Table Insert

1 Square = 1 Stitch

COLOR KEY
772	⊞ Light Green	987	■ Dark Green	807	▲ Blue	208	⊠ Violet
772	◨ Half Cross	349	◉ Dark Coral	741	· Yellow	352	○ Peach

Cross-Stitch Rug

Shown on page 12.

Finished rug is 42½x62½ inches.

MATERIALS
48x68-inch piece of 4-mesh canvas
12 yards of ecru polished cotton
9 printed fabrics of the same weight in colors of your choice in the following amounts: ½ yard *each* for fabrics represented by Nos. 2 and 4 on the Color Key; ¾ yard *each* for fabrics represented by Nos. 1, 3, 6, 7, and 8 in the Color Key; 1 yard for No. 5; and 1½ yards for No. 9
Bookbinder/sailmaker needle, Size 2–4
½-inch bias tape maker (available at fabric and sewing centers)
6 yards of 1-inch-wide finishing tape
1¾ yards of muslin for backing

INSTRUCTIONS
Tear fabric into 1-inch-wide strips; run the strips through the bias tape maker to make ½-inch-wide strips. Fold strips in half lengthwise, edges even, and machine-sew or iron in place.

Before beginning the stitching, refer to the general information on pages 78 and 79. Then begin stitching from chart, *opposite,* at center of design, working cross-stitches over two threads of the canvas. For ease in working, stitch with one strip at a time. Overlap and tack beginning and end of each strip in place when work is completed.

Dampen the piece and block on a flat surface; allow to dry. Press with a hot iron.

On the right side, sew the finishing tape along the edges of the cross-stitching; trim away excess canvas. Turn the taped edge to the wrong side and sew in place.

Cut the muslin to fit the rug, allowing an additional ½ inch all around for seams; press under the seams. With wrong sides facing, pin, then hand-sew the backing to the rug.

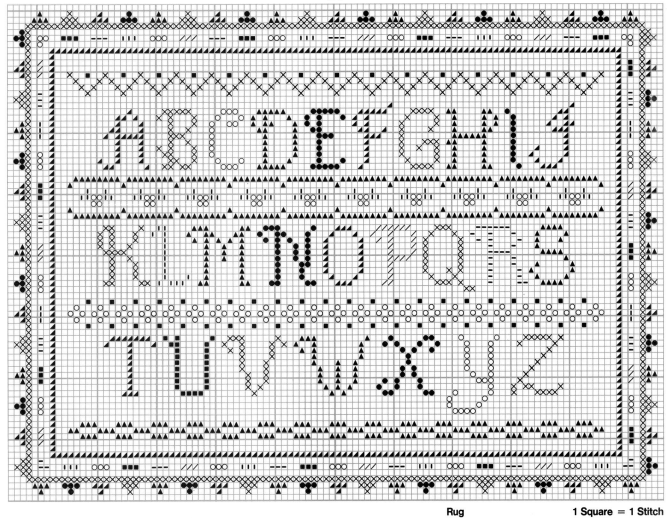

Rug   1 Square = 1 Stitch

COLOR KEY ▯ No. 1 ◼ No. 3 ⊙ No. 5 ◪ No. 7 ▲ No. 9
                ◨ No. 2 ⊟ No. 4 ⊠ No. 6 ⬤ No. 8

"A House Becomes a Home" Sampler

Shown on page 13.

Finished size of framed sampler is 18½x25¼ inches.

MATERIALS
24½x31¼-inch piece of ecru 18-count Davosa cloth
3-ply Paternayan yarn (32-inch lengths) in the following amounts: 14 strands *each* of dark purple (340) and light purple (342); 9 strands of olive green (611); 7 strands of pink (905); 6 strands of red (970); 4 strands *each* of brown (480) and white (260); 2 strands of yellow (773); and 1 strand of tan (473)
DMC embroidery floss: 1 skein of dark brown (3371)
Tapestry needle

INSTRUCTIONS
Before beginning, see the general information on pages 78 and 79 for special cross-stitch tips and techniques, and for materials necessary for working all counted cross-stitch projects.

Referring to the chart on pages 28 and 29, separate the three-ply yarn and use one strand to work cross-stitches over two threads of the fabric.

Measure 3 inches down and 3 inches in from the upper left corner of the fabric; mark this point with a water-erasable pen. Begin stitching there.

Work the heart and tulip border, then stitch the rest of the sampler.

When all cross-stitching is complete, outline the porch and the fence with backstitches, using two strands of brown embroidery floss over two strands of the fabric.

Frame the sampler as desired.

Checkpoints In Your Stitching

As you work your cross-stitch projects, it's wise to periodically check your work to avoid ripping out. This is especially important when working with dark threads on light fabrics, because the dark threads may leave a stain when they're removed.

Examine your work as you complete a section of a design to make sure the cross-stitches are *complete* stitches and the top stitch of the cross is worked in the same direction throughout.

When working a border design, stitch the basics (or the stitches with the lighter threads) of the border first to make sure your counting is accurate, then complete the remaining portions of the border later.

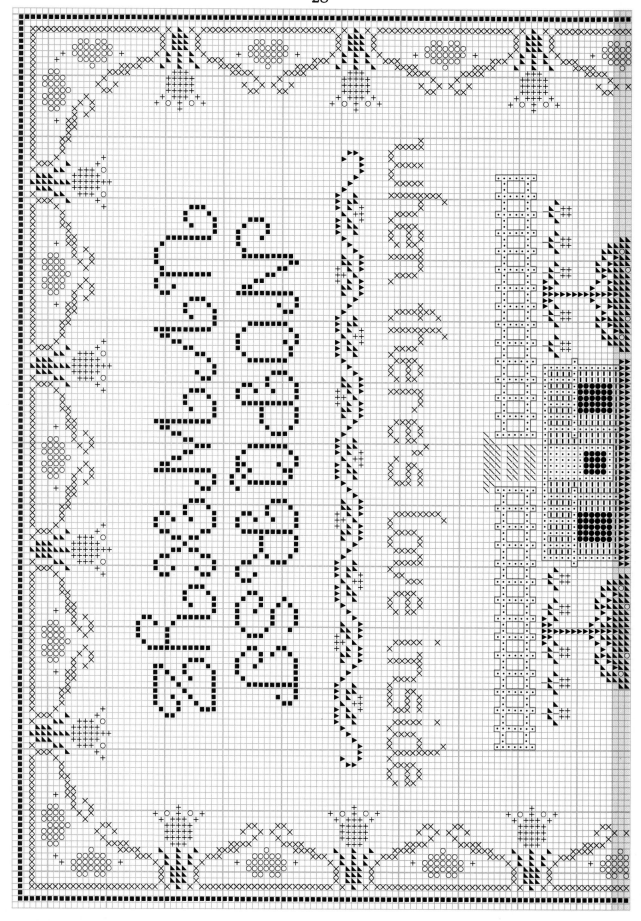

COLOR KEY

340 ■ Dark Purple	611 ◨ Olive Green	970 ○ Red	260 · White	473 ⧄ Tan
342 ⊠ Light Purple	905 ⊞ Pink	480 ▲ Brown	773 ⊟ Yellow	

1 Square = 1 Stitch

3371 ◉ Dark Brown DMC Floss

HEARTS AND FLOWERS

FOR SOMEONE SPECIAL

Here is a veritable garden of delights—
samplers embellished with sweet
words of love, hearts, and flowers such
as roses that represent feelings. The
next time you need a gift for a
close friend or loved one, select one of
the charming designs in this chapter.
You'll enjoy stitching it, and the lucky
recipient of your handiwork is sure
to be touched by your efforts.

The floral alphabet sampler, *right,* is both a gardener's and a stitcher's treasure, for every letter is illustrated with its own motif. Also, because the designs are arranged in a grid, you'll find that stitching this pattern is easy.

You can cross-stitch this 14½x18½-inch sampler on 25-count even-weave fabric using embroidery floss and working over two threads of the fabric. Or, for a slightly larger sampler, substitute hardanger cloth for the finer weave fabric.

This design works up equally well into a spectacular quilt when you stitch the motifs as separate quilt blocks. Simply cross-stitch the patterns onto squares of ecru or white cotton, using waste canvas. Then assemble the quilt with sashing and border strips to accommodate the size of your bed.

Turn the page to discover other quick, creative ways to use elements of this design for special gifts, home accents, and even bazaar best-sellers.

Directions for all the projects in this chapter begin on page 38.

Use the motifs in the sampler on the preceding page to create the projects shown here.

The 17-inch-square pillows, *opposite,* stitched with yarn rather than floss, are a welcome addition to any decor. Make them personal by cross-stitching your own or a friend's initials.

Or, cross-stitch a loved one's name onto needlepoint canvas using ribbons or pearl cotton, then frame the design as shown *below.* (You can craft a bookmark by stitching a name onto hardanger cloth using floss.)

The quick-to-make 3½-inch-square gift tags, *right,* are stitched on perforated paper and framed with bright colored card stock.

HEARTS AND FLOWERS

Tender sentiments and floral motifs that affirm your affection make each of these projects a perfect declaration of heartfelt devotion.

"When love is met ..." is a time-honored romantic verse. Stitch it on hardanger using floss to create the 11⅛x12⅛-inch sampler, *above*.

Or, work just the center motif and sew it into a heart-shape pincushion or sachet. (If you make a sachet, you might want to fill it with potpourri that includes roses and pansies to symbolize love, grace, and beauty.)

The pillow design, *opposite*, with its delicate border, single rose (for simplicity), and yellow violets (for happiness), is as sweet as an old-fashioned valentine. Stitch it into a 16x17-inch pillow as shown.

Or, cross-stitch just the lacy frame onto perforated paper. Then cut out the center of the paper, and turn your stitchery into a picture frame for a favorite photograph.

The "Harmony, unity" sampler, *opposite*, is a lovely pattern for commemorating a special celebration such as a wedding or anniversary. The graceful flowers surrounding the heart symbolize love and purity.

The sampler shown is worked on perforated paper, but the design can be stitched easily onto any even-weave fabric and sewn into a pillow or album cover.

As delicate as woodland blossoms, the cross-stitch design on the box, *above,* makes a beautiful gift for all the romantics you know.

Decorated with hearts and flowers worked in pastel embroidery floss, this 9x9-inch stitchery allows you to add a message in the center of the design or to cross-stitch the initials of the recipient of your gift.

Or, turn the design into a ring bearer's pillow and present it to a bride-to-be. Make the pillow extra-special by working part of the pattern in metallic threads or adding beads and other trims as you stitch.

Bouquets of tulips and lilacs tied with ribbons form the outer borders of the wedding sampler, *opposite.*

The sampler shown is stitched in soft shades of coral and burgundy. But you easily can alter the colors, and work the pattern to fit your own favorites.

To be certain the message for your sampler fits within the wreath, chart it before you begin, using your handwriting or another alphabet from the book.

For a spectacular fashion hit, stitch the pattern using waste canvas onto a blouse or sweater. Pearl cotton or a single ply of crewel yarn is a suitable thread choice for stitching. Then, remove the waste canvas when the stitching is complete.

Amy Larson
and
Brian Lundquist
were wed at ten o'clock
in the morning
on Friday,
August 15, 1986

Flower Sampler - Top Left

COLOR KEY								
	208 ⊠ Lavender	813 ◉ Colonial Blue	350 ⊞ Terra Cotta	309 ◎ Rose
561 ◪ Dark Jade	552 ▲ Purple	726 ⊟ Yellow	957 ⊡ Pink	436 ▼ Golden Brown
554 ■ Orchid	798 ◩ Blue	741 ◌ Gold	3687 ⊗ Plum	414 ◹ Gray

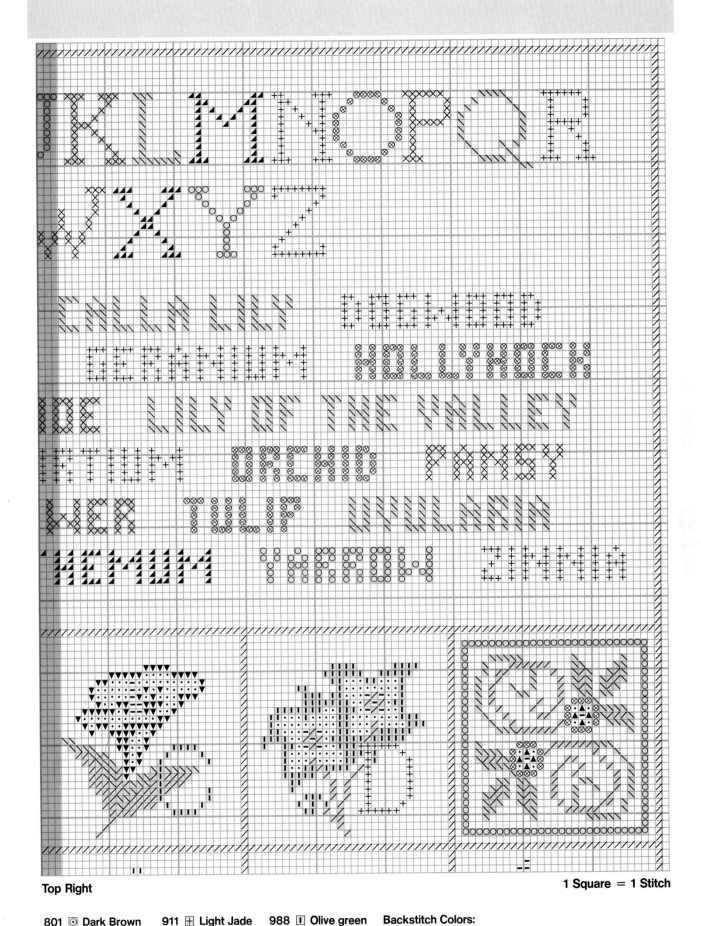

Top Right

1 Square = 1 Stitch

801	◎ Dark Brown	911	⊞ Light Jade	988	▯ Olive green	**Backstitch Colors:**
921	⊠ Rust	993	⊟ Aqua	310	⊡ Black	921 J and Y = Rust	208 P and R = Dark Lavender
991	▱ Teal	906	◳ Lime		⊡ White	310 L = Black	436 U and S = Golden Brown

HEARTS AND FLOWERS

Flower Sampler - Bottom Left

COLOR KEY

208 ⊠ Lavender	813 ● Colonial Blue	350 ⊞ Terra Cotta	309 ◎ Rose
561 ⧄ Dark Jade	552 ▲ Purple	726 − Yellow	957 Ⅰ Pink	436 ▼ Golden Brown
554 ■ Orchid	798 ◢ Blue	741 ◯ Gold	3687 ⊗ Plum	414 ◺ Gray

Bottom Right

801 ⊙ Dark Brown	911 ⊞ Light Jade	988 Ⅰ Olive green	**Backstitch Colors:**	
921 ⊠ Rust	993 ⊟ Aqua	310 ⊡ Black	921 J and Y = Rust	208 P and R = Dark Lavender
991 ⊘ Teal	906 ◨ Lime	⊡ White	310 L = Black	436 U and S = Golden Brown

1 Square = 1 Stitch

Flower Sampler

Shown on pages 30–31.

Finished size of stitched piece is 14½x18½ inches, excluding ⅝-inch borders around stitching.

MATERIALS
20x24-inch piece of 25-count even-weave linen
DMC embroidery floss: 1 skein *each* of the following colors: dark jade (561), light jade (911), orchid (554), dark lavender (208), purple (552), blue (798), colonial blue (813), yellow (726), gold (741), light terra-cotta (350), bright pink (957), plum (3687), deep rose (309), golden brown (436), gray (414), dark brown (801), rust (921), dark teal (991), aqua (993), lime (906), olive green (988), black (310), and white
Tapestry needle

INSTRUCTIONS
Before beginning, see the general information on pages 78 and 79 for special cross-stitch techniques and tips.

Refer to the charts on pages 38–41 for the complete cross-stitch pattern. Use two strands of floss to work cross-stitches over two threads of the fabric. Begin stitching in any corner, 3 inches in from both sides of the fabric, and work the outside border. The border consists of 181 cross-stitches along its width and 231 cross-stitches along its length.

Note: The shaded portions of the charts on pages 39–41 are shown only as a guide to aid you in establishing your place as you work from chart to chart; do not work the shaded areas.

When the outside border is complete, work the alphabet grid. For ease in working, work the bottom row of grids first (W, X, Y, and Z row), then continue to work the grids toward the top of the sampler. *Each* square grid is 31x31 cross-stitches. There will be a total of 30 square grids.

Then work the flowers and letters in each grid following the charts. Locate the center of each grid on the fabric and the center of the flower design; begin stitching there.

Complete the top portion of the design, following the charts on pages 38 and 39.

When all stitching is complete, frame as desired.

Flower Gift Tags

Shown on page 33.

Finished size of the folded tag is 3½x3½ inches.

MATERIALS
4-inch square of perforated paper (for one tag)
DMC embroidery floss in colors of your choice
Tapestry needle
7-inch square of card stock in color of your choice (available at framing and art supply stores)
Crafts knife; glue

INSTRUCTIONS
Select the flower design of your choice from the charts on pages 38–41. Use the corresponding letter for the flower or use any letter appropriate for your tag (the initial of the person receiving the gift, for example) and chart the letter around the flower.

Note: The shaded portions of the charts on pages 39 and 41 are shown only as a guide to aid you in establishing your place in your work as you work from chart to chart. Do not work these areas.

Locate the center of the design and the center of the perforated paper; begin stitching there. Use two strands of floss to work cross-stitches over one block of the paper. Work border in half-cross-stitches to complete the design.

From the card stock, cut a piece measuring 3½x7 inches. Fold it in half and make a sharp crease; open card. Lightly draw ½-inch borders around the front side of the card only and with the crafts knife cut out the center along the drawn lines. Trim, center, and glue the cross-stitch design to the inside of the front of the card.

From the card stock, cut a piece slightly smaller than 3½x3½ inches and glue it to the edges of the back side of card front (do not put glue on the stitched piece).

Flower Pillows

Shown on page 32.

Pillows are 13½x13½inches, excluding ruffle.

MATERIALS
17½x17½-inch piece of cream 14-count Aida cloth
Paternayan 3-ply Persian yarns in colors of your choice
Tapestry needle
1⅔ yards of purchased piping
14½-inch square of cotton fabric for backing
½ yard of 44-inch-wide contrasting cotton fabric for ruffle
Polyester fiberfill

INSTRUCTIONS
Select a flower design from charts on pages 38–41. Locate center of design and Aida cloth and mark both with water-erasable pen; begin stitching there.

Use 2 plies of the Paternayan yarn to work flower design in cross-stitches over six threads of the cloth. Then work the border with half-cross-stitches over six threads of the cloth.

PILLOW ASSEMBLY: With right sides facing, sew the piping three threads away from the border stitches.

For the ruffle, cut three 4½-inch-wide strips. With right sides facing, sew strips together to make a tube. Fold in half, wrong sides facing, having raw edges even; gather to fit top. Sew ruffle atop piping. Trim away excess Aida cloth.

With right sides facing, sew backing to top, leaving an opening for turning. Clip corners; turn and stuff. Sew opening closed.

Personalized Flower Sampler

Shown on page 33.

Finished size, framed, is 9½x33 inches.

MATERIALS
13x36 inches of 10-count needlepoint canvas for five-letter name (adjust *width* to allow 6 inches for each letter, plus an additional 3 inches on each side for borders)
⅛-inch-wide C.M. Offray ribbons in colors of your choice, allowing 1⅔ yards for working cross-stitches over 1 square inch of canvas
Blunt-end needle

INSTRUCTIONS
Select the flowers for *each* letter in your name from the charts on pages 38–41.

Beginning in the upper right-hand corner, 3 inches down and 3 inches in from the outside edge of the canvas, work the outline borders for each flower block with *half-crosses* over two threads of the canvas. Each complete block is 31x31 stitches over 62 threads.

Note: The shaded portions of the charts on pages 39 and 41 are shown only as a guide to aid you in establishing your place as you work from chart to chart. Do not work the shaded areas.

Locate the center of the first flower design in your name and center of the first canvas block. Work the flower design in *cross-stitches*, working each cross-stitch over two threads of the canvas. Repeat these instructions for each of the flower designs to complete your name.

When stitching is complete, frame as desired.

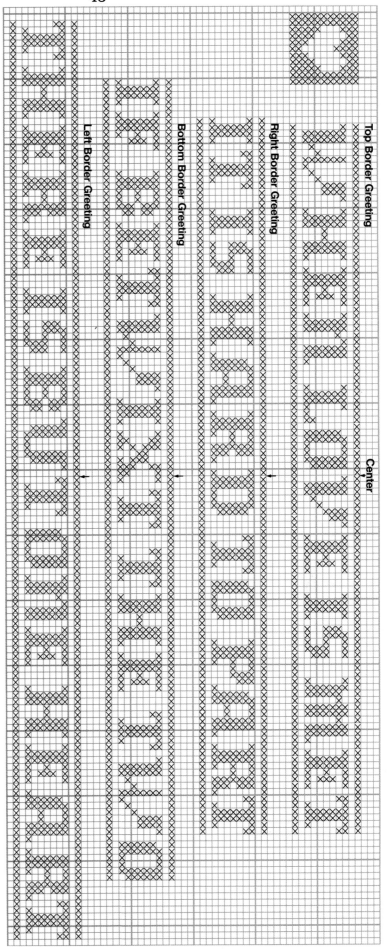

Sayings for "When Love is Met" Sampler

HEARTS AND FLOWERS

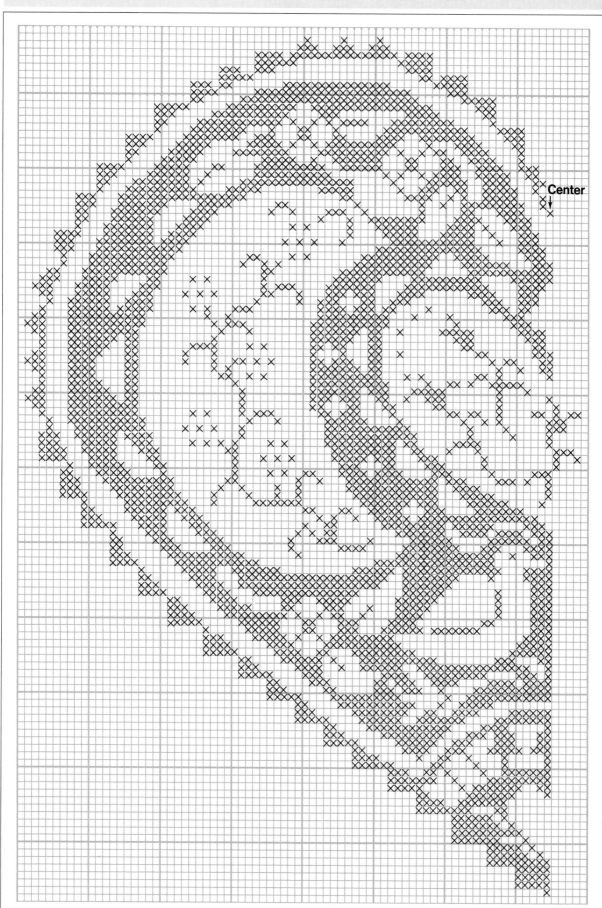

Center

"When Love is Met" Sampler

1 Square = 1 Stitch

Center

Center →

"True Love" Pillow

1 Square = 1 Stitch

COLOR KEY

988 ◪ Green   311 ▣ Navy
335 ⊞ Rose   727 ◉ Yellow
776 ◪ Pink   ⊠ White

"When Love Is Met" Sampler

Shown on page 34.

Finished size of framed sampler is 11⅛x12⅛ inches.

MATERIALS
15x16-inch piece of navy blue hardanger fabric
DMC embroidery floss, 2 skeins of ecru (712)
Tapestry needle

INSTRUCTIONS
Before beginning, see the general information on pages 78 and 79 for special cross-stitch tips and techniques, and for materials necessary for working all counted cross-stitch projects.
Baste lines along the horizontal and vertical centers of the fabric. Then baste lines to establish a rectangle 209 stitches wide by 177 stitches high (be sure to keep rectangle in center of fabric and corresponding with the horizontal and vertical bastings).
Referring to the chart on page 44, locate the center of the heart motif and the fabric; begin stitching there. Using one strand of floss, stitch the design over one thread of the fabric. Work mirror image of the design to complete the center motif.
Work cross-stitches over the rectangular basting thread for the outside border. Then work the inner border with cross-stitches so there are nine stitches *free* between outer and inner borders. Work the small heart motif as shown on chart, page 43, in each corner.
For greetings, locate the center of *each* border band on the fabric and mark with a water-erasable pen. Locate the center of each greeting on chart, page 43, and begin stitching there. The bottom of each border greeting runs along the inside border band; the line of verse on bottom of stitchery is worked upside down. (See photograph, page 34, as a guide.)
Frame sampler as desired.

"True Love" Pillow

Shown on page 35.

Finished size of pillow is 16x17 inches.

MATERIALS
18x18-inch piece of light blue hardanger fabric
DMC embroidery floss, 1 skein *each* of the following colors: green (988), rose (335), pink (776), navy (311), yellow (727), and white
¾ yard of contrasting fabric for backing and borders
2 yards of purchased piping
Polyester fiberfill
Graph paper

INSTRUCTIONS
Before beginning, see the general information on pages 78 and 79 for special cross-stitch tips and techniques, and for the materials necessary for working all counted cross-stitch projects.
Referring to the chart, page 45, transfer the border and center design to graph paper. Flop border to make the mirror images in the remaining three quadrants to complete the design.
Locate the center of the design and the center of the fabric and begin stitching there. Use two strands of floss to work cross-stitches over two threads of fabric. Work all backstitches around the ribbon banner with navy over two threads of the fabric.

PILLOW ASSEMBLY: From the contrasting fabric, cut four 2-inch-wide strips, *each* 17 inches long. Center and sew the strips to the cross-stitch piece, 2¼ inches from the outside of the cross-stitch design, using ½-inch seam allowances. (Miter corners, if desired, for a nicer appearance.)
With right sides facing, sew the piping atop the pillow front along the fabric borders.

Cut pillow backing to fit pillow front. With right sides facing, sew back to front, using ½-inch seams; leave an opening for turning. Clip corners, turn, and stuff; sew opening closed.

"Harmony and Unity" Sampler

Shown on page 35.

Finished size of stitched area is approximately 7x9¼ inches.

MATERIALS
12x18-inch piece of perforated paper
DMC embroidery floss, 1 skein *each* of the following colors: red (304), green (367), blue (931), and coral (760)
Graph paper
Colored pencils
Tapestry needle

INSTRUCTIONS
Before beginning, see the general information on pages 78 and 79 for special cross-stitch tips and techniques, and for materials necessary for working all counted cross-stitch projects.
Referring to the chart on page 47, transfer the design to graph paper. Chart the design with colored pencils to make your work easier when you stitch. Reverse the left-hand side of the heart and vines and add the appropriate year to the chart to complete the date.
Locate the center of the paper and the center of the design on the chart; begin stitching there.
Taking special care to avoid tearing the paper as you stitch, use two strands of floss to work cross-stitches over one square of the paper.
Frame as desired.

Harmony and Unity Sampler

1 Square = 1 Stitch

COLOR KEY
304 ■ Red
367 ■ Green
931 ■ Blue
760 □ Coral

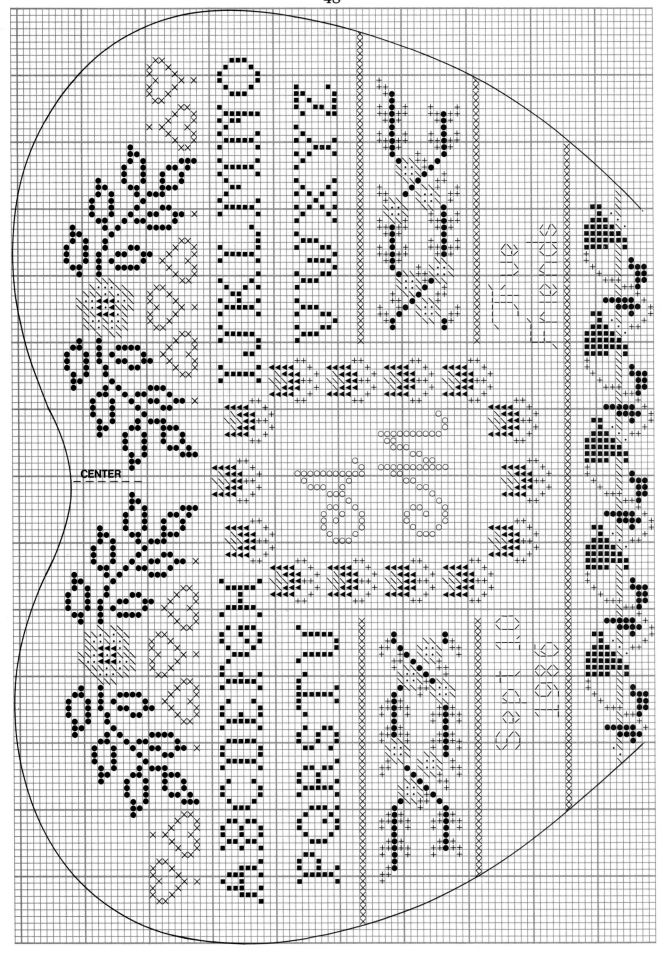

CENTER

Hearts and Flowers Jewelry Box

Shown on page 36.

Finished size of stitched piece, excluding lace, is 7x7½ inches.

MATERIALS
12x12-inch square of 18-count white Aida cloth
DMC embroidery floss: 1 skein *each* of peach (352), dark heather (3041), light heather (3042), evergreen (890), olive green (320), rose (3687), yellow (3078), and blue (597)
Tapestry needle
¾ yard of 1-inch-wide pregathered white lace
¾ yard of burgundy piping
Heart-shape box with a 7x7½-inch heart inset (available at crafts shops or by writing to Plain 'n' Fancy, Inc., Box 357, Mathews, VA 23109)
Water-erasable pen
Polyester batting

INSTRUCTIONS
Before beginning, see the general information on pages 78 and 79 for special cross-stitch tips and techniques, and for materials necessary for working all counted cross-stitch projects.

Chart your initials in the center of the chart, page 48, selecting letters from one of the alphabets in other projects given in the book.

Chart the appropriate month, date, and year in place, using the pattern as a guide or any other special message to personalize your stitchery.

Locate the center of the design and the center of the fabric; begin stitching there. (The chart on page 49 is a continuation of the chart on page 48. Use both of these charts to find the center of the work.)

Note: The shaded portions of the chart on page 49 are shown only as a guide to aid you in establishing your place as you work from chart to chart. Do not work the shaded areas.

Use two strands of floss to work cross-stitches over one thread of the fabric. Work the date and greeting with backstitches over one thread of the fabric with two strands of evergreen floss.

When the stitchery is complete, press the piece on the wrong side using a warm iron.

ASSEMBLING THE BOX: Remove the insert on the lid of the box. Discard the heart-shape foam, if desired, and replace it with two or three layers of heart-shape batting taped to the wooden insert. Discard the muslin piece.

Lay the wooden heart insert *atop* the stitchery, right side up. Using a water-erasable pen, draw the heart outline onto the fabric to establish a sewing line. With right sides facing, baste, then sew the burgundy piping to the sewing line. Lay the lace edging atop the piping and sew through all thicknesses. Trim the excess Aida cloth about 1 inch from seam line. Clip into the 1-inch seam allowance about every ½ inch.

With right side up, center the stitchery over the heart insert. Fold excess fabric to the back and tape in place. *Note:* Do not cover the holes on the insert for the mounting screws.

Mount the heart insert to the box, following the manufacturer's directions.

CENTER

COLOR KEY

3041 ◼ Dark Heather	3687 ▲ Rose		
3042 ◻ Light Heather	352 ◿ Peach		
890 ◉ Evergreen	597 ⊠ Blue		
320 ⊞ Olive Green	3078 · Yellow		

1 Square = 1 Stitch

HEARTS AND FLOWERS

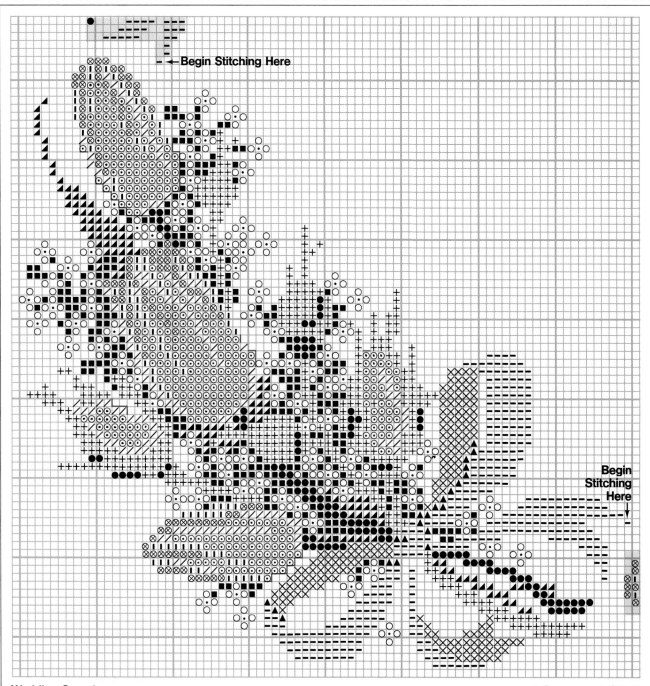

← Begin Stitching Here

Begin Stitching Here

Wedding Sampler

1 Square = 1 Stitch

COLOR KEY

553 ▣ Dark Purple	3685 ▲ Dark Burgundy	367 ◪ Dark Green	3328 ⊠ Dark Coral
554 ◯ Light Purple	3687 ⊠ Medium Burgundy	368 ● Medium Green	760 ⊘ Medium Coral
745 · Yellow	3688 − Light Burgundy	369 ⊞ Light Green	761 I Light Coral
754 ◎ Peach			

Wedding Sampler

Shown on page 37.

Finished size of the framed sampler is 19½x19½ inches.

MATERIALS
16x16-inch piece of cream 14-count Aida cloth
DMC embroidery floss: 1 skein *each* of dark green (367), medium green (368), light green (369), dark burgundy (3685), medium burgundy (3687), light burgundy (3688), yellow (745), dark purple (553), light purple (554), peach (754), light coral (761), medium coral (760), and dark coral (3328)
Tapestry needle; graph paper

INSTRUCTIONS
Before beginning, see the general information on pages 78 and 79 for special cross-stitch tips and techniques.

The chart on page 50 represents just one-fourth of the border design. For ease in working the pattern, transfer the design to graph paper. Use colored pencils to make your stitching easier. Flop the border to make the mirror images in the remaining three quadrants. *Note:* The shaded areas on the chart indicate the placements of the beginning and ending of each succeeding design as it encircles the chart.

Using your handwriting or an alphabet from another project in this book, chart onto the graph paper the announcement for your sampler. If you use your handwriting, work this lettering with backstitches. Complete the announcement on the graph paper before beginning the stitching to ensure proper placement.

Begin stitching the design 4 inches from the center of the bottom edge of the fabric. *Note:* The arrow on the chart indicates where stitching begins. Use two strands of floss to work each cross-stitch over one square of the Aida cloth.

Frame as desired.

Creating Your Own Cross-Stitch Designs

Even if designing isn't your forte, you still can create lovely stitchery with a personal touch by collecting cross-stitch motifs and arranging them until you've achieved a pleasing design. The tips below will help you create cross-stitch originals for yourself, your family, and friends.

Collecting patterns: Begin by browsing through current crafts books and magazines. Watch for needlepoint, filet crochet, and fair isle knitting patterns, too, because these patterns translate easily into cross-stitch designs.

Clip motifs that you like, or copy them onto graph paper. Search for old pattern books and stitcheries at antique shops and garage sales. Look through coloring and other children's books for design possibilities. Then convert these to cross-stitch patterns by laying the picture atop a light box (or in a window), placing graph paper over the picture, and charting the area with crosses.

Organizing designs: Place patterns between acetate sheets for protection and store them in a ring binder.

For your convenience and easy reference, divide the patterns into sections labeled by subject matter—alphabets, borders, animals, Christmas motifs, flowers, and any other subject area that fits your personal taste.

Charting patterns: As special occasions approach, pull out the binder and select motifs that are appropriate. If a name or message is included, chart this first; then place the motifs in a pleasing arrangement around the message.

It's easiest to design patterns with a repeat motif. For a pillow, start with a quarter of the total design; complete it by making mirror images in the remaining three sections. The pillow on page 45 and the bridal sampler, *opposite,* are examples of this kind of patterning.

Create a picture similarly, except design half of the chart and flop it to complete the mirror image. The Harmony and Unity sampler pattern on page 47 and the Heart sampler on page 44 are examples of this type of design.

To make a sampler, chart out an alphabet, a message, and then your name. Select some of your favorite motifs, such as small flowers, hearts, or some interesting leaf patterns and arrange them around your lettering. Then establish a simple border to hold your sampler together. Keep in mind that most samplers are very linear and need not be complex.

Stitching your design: Remember that your design on graph paper will not be the finished size of your work; in most cases, the design will be considerably larger on paper. Determine the finished size of your stitchery before you begin purchasing your materials and stitching.

Count the number of stitches and empty spaces across both the width and the length of your chart. Then consider the stitching options: When you work with 14-count Aida cloth and work over one thread of the cloth, you will have either 14 stitches or spaces, or combinations of both, for every inch of stitching.

If you use hardanger, with 22 threads per inch, and stitch over one thread, your finished piece will be considerably smaller than when you stitch on Aida cloth. Or you might stitch over two threads of the hardanger; your piece will be twice as large as when you stitch over one thread of the same cloth.

The selection of the number of threads of embroidery floss, or the use of pearl cotton, persian yarns, ribbons, or other yarns or threads can affect the finished appearance and size of your stitched piece. Experiment with all the possibilities before beginning your work.

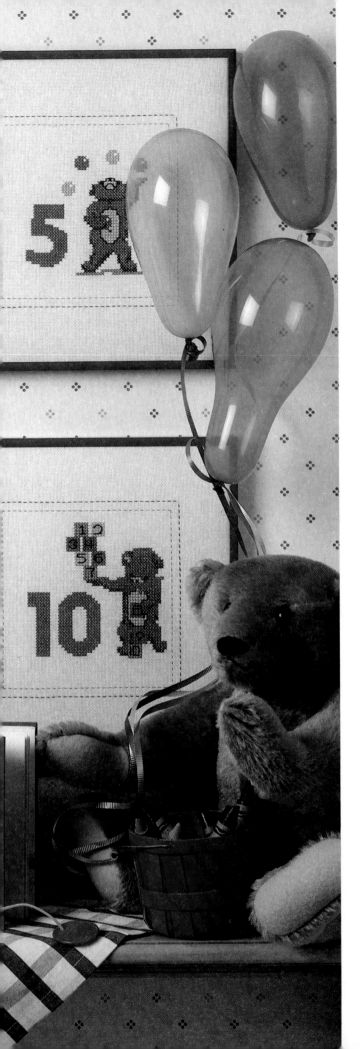

FANCIFUL TREASURES

Whether you stitch the projects in this section for a child's room or for moments of quiet play, these charming patterns are sure to please youngsters of all ages. You'll also find that the sampler designs will inspire dozens of other enchanting and imaginative cross-stitch projects.

What child could resist the whimsical counting bears in the samplers, *left*. Each of the numbers is illustrated with a kid-pleasing activity.

To make this design for your own favorite child, stitch 6-inch-square blocks onto hardanger fabric using embroidery floss. Then arrange them into two 10¼x33½-inch samplers (or another shape of your own choosing). The samplers will brighten a child's room and help him or her learn his numbers at the same time.

Or, for a child's coverlet, work the designs onto 7-inch squares of hardanger fabric and assemble them into quilt blocks using your favorite patchwork techniques. (You might border each block with sashing strips in bright colors.) If you need additional blocks to complete the quilt, appliqué letters or hearts onto squares of complementary fabrics.

Directions for all the projects in this section begin on page 62. Please turn the page for more ideas for using these teddy bear designs.

FANCIFUL TREASURES

These delightful projects, based on the sampler shown on pages 52 and 53, will warm the hearts of little ones.

Turn those playful bears into a soft, washable book, as shown *below,* and introduce a toddler to the pleasures of reading.

The pages of our book are stitched onto pastel shades of Aida cloth using pearl cotton threads. You can easily stitch them onto *any* light-colored cotton fabric using waste canvas. In the instructions you'll find charts for the lettering that accompanies each teddy bear number.

Cover your book (and make it completely washable) with a bright plaid or calico fabric.

Make a child's birthday memorable with the 11¾x14¼-inch birthday sampler, *opposite,* stitched on perforated paper using embroidery floss. You can adapt the chart to fit the age of your child simply by changing the large number and the number of candles on the cake. Then, to personalize the sampler, stitch your child's name at the top and birth date at the bottom of the picture.

Another creative way to use these designs is to stitch them onto your children's clothing—the bib of a pinafore or overalls, for example— to make the clothes playtime favorites.

Christie Anne

HAPPY
BIRTHDAY

8

October 15, 1

Nothing pleases children more than having their names or other special trims on their possessions. So why not stitch a sampler onto a purchased chair the next time you need a personal, sure-to-please present for a toddler. (The source for the chairs is included in the acknowledgments, page 80.)

Simply work the stitching atop the mesh canvas seats with any materials that are heavy enough to show the design. You'll find you can complete these projects in practically no time.

For the rocker, we used wool embroidery yarns; for the director's chair, we used narrow ribbons. Sport or crewel yarns or gimp would be equally effective.

You also might adapt these designs to fit a child's pillowcase or favorite blanket—then nap time will be a choreless activity for Mom.

FANCIFUL TREASURES

FANCIFUL TREASURES

The shaped pillow toys, *opposite,* and the sampler, *right,* are sparkling accents for a newborn's nursery. Stitch the motifs and borders before the baby's birth, then add the personal information after the baby arrives.

Both the lamb and the bear are stitched onto hardanger fabric using embroidery floss. Unclipped turkey work (a knotted stitch) in sport yarn creates the fluffy head of the lamb. A satin bow and two buttons accent the bear's attire when the cross-stitching is complete.

For the 10x12-inch birth announcement, *right,* two teddy bears— one studious and one at play—flank the baby's name and date of birth. Stitch the sampler over one thread of Aida cloth using embroidery floss. Or, double the size of the picture by working over two threads of the fabric.

Here's a plaything to stitch for a special child and then, when she has outgrown it (if she ever does), set it aside for *her* child someday. This unusually pretty doll is sure to please generations of children.

Craft this 21½-inch-tall young lady on hardanger cloth, embellishing her torso with a stitched-on camisole complete with ruffles and bows (see photo, *opposite*).

Then sew a bonnet and pretty prairie-style dress. Top the dress with a cross-stitch pinafore, *above*, adorned with hearts and flowers, an alphabet, the child's name, your own name (or "Mommy" or "Grandma"), and the year in which you created (and bestowed) this elegant gift.

Why not stitch a look-alike pinafore for your youngster as well (*opposite*), trimming it with all the motifs that appear on the doll's outfit. You'll find directions for the child-size pinafore along with those for the doll.

Teddy Bear Patterns

1 Square = 1 Stitch

1 Square = 1 Stitch

COLOR KEY

300 ■ Dark Brown	666 ◉ Red	703 ⊞ Green	738 ⊟ Beige	3688 Ⅱ Rose
301 ⊠ Light Brown	798 ▲ Blue	310 ◪ Black	972 ⊡ Yellow	310 ■ Black

Teddy Bear Counting Sampler

Shown on pages 52–53.

Finished size, framed, of each sampler is 10¼x33½ inches.

MATERIALS
2 pieces of white hardanger, *each* measuring 14x37 inches
DMC embroidery floss in the following amounts and colors:
2 skeins *each* of red (666) and light brown (301); 1 skein *each* of green (703), rose (3688), yellow (972), blue (798), dark brown (300), beige (738), and black (310)
Tapestry needle

INSTRUCTIONS
Before beginning, see the general information on pages 78 and 79 for special cross-stitch tips and techniques, and for materials necessary for working all counted cross-stitch projects.

Note: The "1" block on the chart, *opposite,* indicates the full size for all the blocks. The design center of all the blocks is marked with an arrow. Use this marking to determine the center of each of the designs on the fabric.

Locate the center of the fabric's width and run a basting thread through the center of the fabric. Locate the center of the "1" block ("6" block for the second sampler) and begin stitching there, 6½ inches from the edge of the left-hand side of the fabric. Use two strands of floss to work the cross-stitches over two threads of the fabric.

continued

Work the inside border stitches around the "1" and "6" blocks, with running stitches in blue over two threads of the fabric. *Each* block has 31 running stitches over the top of the fabric and 30 stitches under the fabric on *each* side. Begin each stitch at each corner with a running stitch over the top of the fabric (at each corner there will be two consecutive running stitches over the top of the fabric).

Leave six threads between *each* block as you work to the right of each finished block to add the re-maining blocks. For ease in work-ing, stitch the border stitches of each succeeding block as you work to the right, then locate the center of the fabric block and the center of the design and begin stitching there. The border stitch-es of the "2" and "7" are worked with yellow; "3" and "8" are worked with red; "4" and "9" are worked with green; and "5" and "10" are worked with rose.

Work the backstitches for each of the blocks as follows: *For all the bears:* Outline the eyes and work the mouth with black. Out-line the teddy bear tummy and muzzle using dark brown.

For the "1" block: Work the kite strings with black and the kite tails with red. *For the "2" block:* Work the butterfly antennae with dark brown and the catcher with black. *For the "3" block:* Work all the door trim with dark brown and the key chain with black. *For the "4" block:* Work the balloon strings with black. *For the "6" block:* Work the tree trunk with dark brown and the apple stems with green. *For the "7" block:* Work the fishing line with black and the water with blue. *For the "8" block:* Work as for the Birth-day Sampler, page 65. *For the "9" block:* Work the bubbles in pastel shades of rose, yellow, and blue. *For the "10" block:* Work all the numbers in the playing blocks with black.

When all the blocks are com-pleted, skip six strands of the fab-ric and stitch the outside border with red using running stitches. On the border, align the stitching with the border stitches of the blocks, keeping the over and un-der stitches parallel to the border stitches of the blocks (the corners will have no running stitches).

Frame samplers as desired.

Teddy Bear Counting Book

Shown on page 54.

Finished size of the book is 11¼ x 13½ inches.

MATERIALS
For the pages
14x24-inch pieces of 14-count Aida cloth in the following amounts: Three pieces of pink; one piece *each* of light blue, yellow, and green
DMC Size 3 pearl cotton, red (666), light brown (976), green (703), rose (899), yellow (972), blue (798), dark brown (801), beige (738), and black (310)
Graph paper
Rickrack in pastel colors (1¼ yards for each page)
Tapestry needle

Teddy Bear Counting Book

1 Square = 1 Stitch

COLOR KEY   666 ⊠ Red

For the cover
⅞ yard of striped, plaid, or print fabric for the cover and cover facing

½ yard of backing fabric

2¼ yards of purchased piping in color of your choice

½ yard of fusible interfacing

INSTRUCTIONS
To make the book pages

Locate the center of all the written lines for the book, *opposite,* and the center of all the bear patterns, pages 62 and 63. Using graph paper, center and chart the written line onto the appropriate bear pattern. Allow 20 squares between the bottom line of the number on the bear design and the top of the capital letter of the written line.

Run a basting thread through the center of each of the Aida cloth pieces, both horizontally and vertically. Then run two more basting threads, vertically, to divide each of the pieces into eight equal parts. You now have established two pages with the center fold line between each of these pages for each piece of Aida cloth.

Locate the center of the bear patterns (with the written words), and begin stitching the designs in the center of *one* of the pages (two designs will be worked on one piece of Aida cloth). Work cross-stitches with one strand of pearl cotton over two squares of the Aida cloth. See the Teddy Bear Counting Sampler, *opposite,* for instructions for working the backstitches of each design.

For paging sequence, stitch the designs on the pages as follows, working the first number cited on the left side of the cloth and the second number on the right side of the cloth: Stitch the number "1" and "10" designs on the blue cloth; the "9" and "2" on the pink; the "3" and "8" on the yellow; the "7" and "4" on the pink; and the "5" and "6" on the green. One piece of pink is unworked.

Trim all the pages to measure 13½x22½ inches, making sure the stitched designs are centered on each half-page, with approximately 2-inch borders all around.

Sew rickrack around each design to frame each page to measure 10x11¾ inches.

Allowing ½ inch for seam allowances, and with right sides facing, sew the unworked pink piece to the blue page, leaving an opening for turning; stitch the pink "9 and 2" page to the yellow page; stitch the pink "7 and 4" page to the green page. Trim seams; turn, press, and sew openings closed.

To make the book cover

From striped or print fabric, batting, and backing fabric, cut a rectangle measuring 15½x28 inches from each fabric.

Place batting between the backing and striped fabric and baste through all thicknesses; quilt as desired. Trim the quilted piece to measure 13¾x23¼ inches. Then baste and sew the piping ¼ inch from edge of quilted top.

Cut another piece of striped fabric to fit the quilted piece and fuse it with the interfacing to the wrong side.

Allowing ¼-inch seam allowances, with right sides facing, sew quilted and fused pieces together. Leave opening for turning; turn, press, and sew opening closed.

Open cover, center assembled pages in numerical order, and sew through all thicknesses on the center line to assemble the book. Remove all bastings.

Happy Birthday Bear Sampler

Shown on page 55.

Finished size of framed picture is 11¾x14¼ inches.

MATERIALS
12x18-inch piece of perforated paper

DMC embroidery floss: 1 skein *each* of dark brown (300), medium brown (301), beige (738), blue (798), red (666), and black (310); scraps of yellow (972), rose (3688), and green (905)

Tapestry needle; graph paper

INSTRUCTIONS

Refer to the birthday bear pattern on page 63. Chart pattern onto graph paper and change the numeral and the number of candles on the cake to match the age of the birthday child. Use an alphabet from other patterns in the book to chart name and date. Allow 11 rows of squares between the name and the candle flames, and 9 rows between the "O" in October (or the first letter of the appropriate month) and the bottom row of grass.

Locate the center of the pattern and the center of the perforated paper; begin stitching there. Use four strands of floss to work all stitching. Work each cross-stitch, half cross-stitch, and backstitch over two squares of the paper.

Embroider the cross-stitches first, then work the half cross-stitches and backstitches.

For the teddy bear: Outline the eyes, towel, and mouth with black backstitches. Outline the bear tummy and muzzle using dark brown backstitches.

For the cake: Embroider the candle flames using yellow half cross-stitches. Work "HAPPY BIRTHDAY" using red backstitches. Outline the cake with blue backstitches.

Frame the stitchery as desired.

Sampler Chairs For Toddlers

Shown on pages 56–57.

MATERIALS
For the rocker
Tyke-Hike™ rocker

3-ply Paternayan yarn: 2 strands *each* of red, blue, green, and lavender; 1 strand of orange

Large-eye tapestry needle

For the director's chair
Tyke-Hike™ chair

1/16-inch-wide ribbon: 13 yards of green, 9½ yards of red, 7 yards *each* of lavender and orange, and 4½ yards of blue

Large-eye tapestry needle

continued

INSTRUCTIONS
For the rocker

Before beginning, see the general information on pages 78 and 79 for special cross-stitch tips and techniques, and for materials necessary for working all counted cross-stitch projects.

Referring to the chart, *below, bottom,* use one ply of yarn to work cross-stitches over three "threads" of the plastic. Locate the center of the width at the bottom of the rocker's back. Count up 22 holes from this point and begin working the cross-stitches with the row of blue numbers.

For the director's chair

Cut the ribbon into 48-inch lengths and work cross-stitches over two "threads" of the plastic following the chart, *below, top.*

Locate the center of the width on the chair seat; measure 1¼ inches up from the lower edge of the seat. Locate the center of the width on the bottom of the pattern. Begin stitching with the green border row. Complete border, then work center design, filling in the child's name and appropriate year. *Note:* The ribbon cross-stitches should lie flat against the canvas.

Lamb Pillow

Shown on page 58.

Finished size of pillow is approximately 14x16 inches.

MATERIALS
18x20-inch piece of white hardanger fabric
DMC embroidery floss in the following amounts and colors: 2 skeins of pink (776); 1 skein *each* of rose (3687), purple (208), aqua (518), peach (3341), yellow (726), and green (772)
Tapestry needle
Scraps of white sport yarn
¾ yard of calico fabric for backing and piping
2½ yards of narrow cotton cording
Polyester fiberfill

INSTRUCTIONS
For the embroidery

Before beginning, see the general information on pages 78 and 79 for special cross-stitch tips and techniques, and for materials necessary for working all counted cross-stitch projects.

Using an alphabet and numbers from other projects in this book, chart the child's name and birth date in the blank area between the flower and heart borders on the chart, *opposite.*

Locate the center of the design and the center of the fabric; mark with a water-erasable pen; begin stitching there. Use two threads of the floss to work the cross-stitches over three threads of the hardanger fabric. Use sport yarn to fill in the top of the head with unclipped turkey work embroidery stitches when cross-stitching is complete.

To assemble the pillow

With the water-erasable pen, draw outline of the shaped lamb 1½ inches from the outside row of stitches (includes ½-inch seam allowance). Cut along this line. Cut a piece to match the cut piece from the calico fabric for backing.

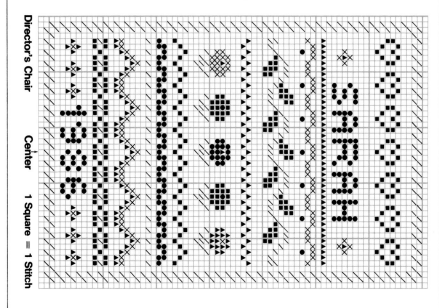

Director's Chair   Center   1 Square = 1 Stitch

COLOR KEY
970 ■ Red		542 ⊠ Blue
301 ◉ Lavender		621 ▢ Green
821 ▣ Orange		

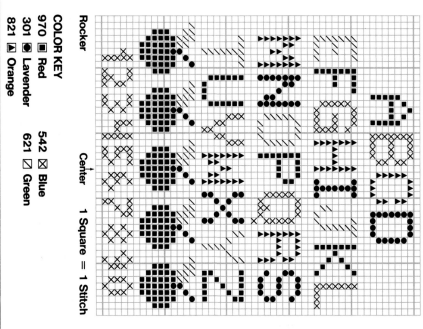

Rocker   Center   1 Square = 1 Stitch

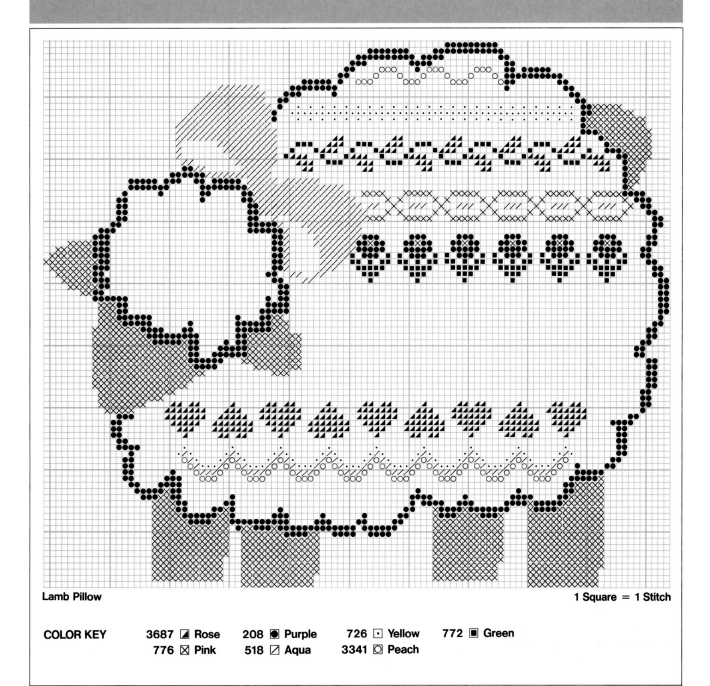

Lamb Pillow

1 Square = 1 Stitch

COLOR KEY   3687 ◪ Rose   208 ⬤ Purple   726 ⊡ Yellow   772 ▣ Green

776 ⊠ Pink   518 ◹ Aqua   3341 ⊙ Peach

Cut 1½-inch-wide bias strips of calico and sew together in one long strip. With zipper foot, cover the cording with the strip of calico to make the piping. Baste, then sew the piping along the ½-inch seam allowance; clip corners and around curved edges.

With right sides together, sew backing to cross-stitched piece, leaving an opening for turning. Clip curves; turn and stuff. Sew opening closed.

Teddy Bear Doll

Shown on page 58.

Finished size is 18½ inches tall.

MATERIALS
22x24-inch piece of white hardanger
DMC embroidery floss: 4 skeins of brown (400); 2 skeins of dark blue (798); and 1 skein *each* of light blue (3325), yellow (744), green (563), dark peach (352), light peach (353), dark lavender (208), light lavender (554), dark pink (891), and light pink (3708)
Tapestry needle
Water-erasable pen
22x22-inch square of fleece
¾ yard of blue pindot fabric for backing
2½ yards of blue cotton piping
½ yard of 1-inch-wide red grosgrain ribbon
Two ⅞-inch-diameter blue buttons
Polyester fiberfill

continued

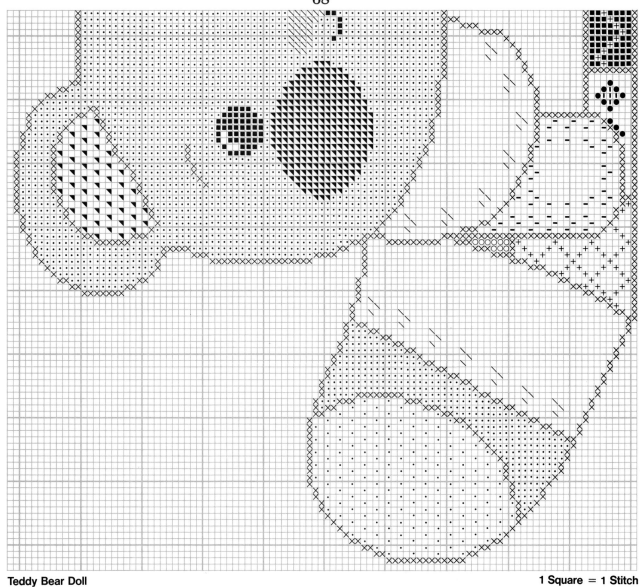

Teddy Bear Doll

1 Square = 1 Stitch

COLOR KEY

798 ⊠ Dark Blue	554 ⊟ Light Lavender	352 ⊡ Dark Peach	563 ⊞ Green
3325 ▣ Light Blue	891 ◪ Dark Pink	353 ◨ Light Peach	744 ◯ Yellow
208 ◉ Dark Lavender	3708 ◢ Light Pink	400 · Brown	

INSTRUCTIONS

Cross-stitching the teddy bear

Referring to the chart, *above,* for the teddy bear pattern, and the photograph, page 58, personalize the initial "boxes" on the overalls, if desired. Fill boxes with baby's weight and birth date. Other information—baby's name, time of birth, and names of parents and grandparents, for example—can be added by eliminating patterns within any of the boxes. Refer to other alphabets in patterns throughout the book for charting.

Refer to the photograph, page 58, when working the opposite side of the bear's overalls. The designs within the boxes are staggered throughout. Select designs and use colors of your choice to stitch the patterns on the opposite side of the overalls *only.* All other stitching on the bear (head, collar, arms, and feet) is a repeat of the charted design.

Use two strands of embroidery floss to work the cross-stitches and backstitches over two threads of the hardanger fabric.

Locate the center of both the pattern and the fabric; mark the fabric center using a water-erasable pen. Begin stitching the piece at this point, starting with the dark blue cross-stitches on the overalls. For ease in working, stitch all the dark blue cross-stitches that *outline* the bear's shapes. Then, cross-stitch the remaining portions of the bear, filling in the details of arms, legs, face, and overalls.

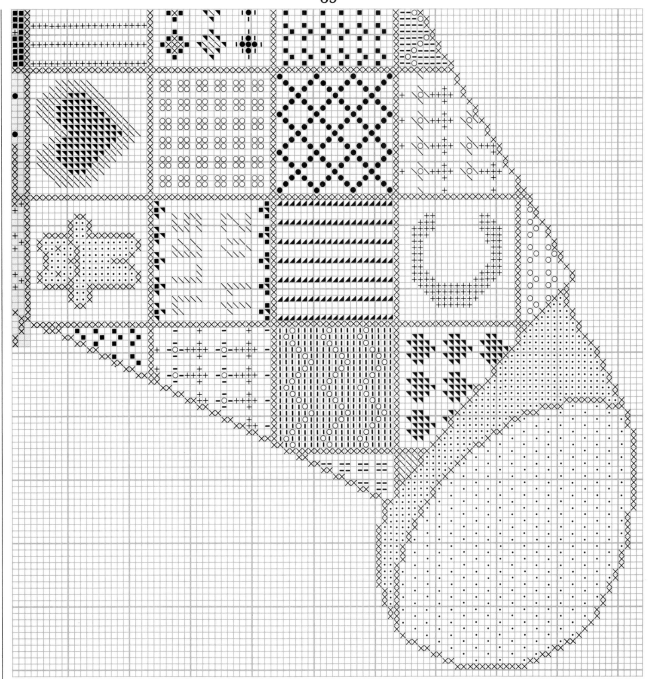

1 Square = 1 Stitch

When all of the cross-stitching is complete, work backstitches to outline facial features using dark blue floss.

Assembling the teddy bear

Sew fleece to wrong side of stitchery, ¼ inch from outside row of cross-stitching. (This will be the sewing guide for stitching the piping.) With right sides to-gether, sew piping along stitching line using zipper foot; clip piping seams at corners and curves.

Stitch buttons to straps of over-alls and tie ribbon into bow and sew along neckline edge.

From blue backing fabric, cut a 24x24-inch square; cut square in half on the straight grain. With right sides together and using ½-inch seams, sew fabric halves to-gether, leaving a 7-inch opening in the center (for ease in stuffing the bear). Press seam open.

With right side of bear centered on right side of backing, sew the two pieces together, using the piping stitching as a guideline. Trim excess fabric ¼ inch from seam line. Clip seam allowance every ⅛ inch. Turn, press, and stuff with fiberfill. Slip-stitch opening closed.

Teddy Bear Birth Sampler

1 Square = 1 Stitch

COLOR KEY

	351	Orange	989	Light Olive	993	Mint Green
776	Pink	422	Beige	825	Dark Blue	975	Brown
309	Rose	742	Yellow	807	Light Blue		

Backstitching

898 Dark Brown
413 Charcoal

FANCIFUL TREASURES

Teddy Bear Birth Sampler

Shown on page 59.

Finished size, framed, is 10x12½ inches.

MATERIALS
13x16-inch piece of 14-count white Aida cloth
DMC embroidery floss: 1 skein *each* of dark blue (825), light blue (807), brown (975), beige (422), light olive (989), yellow (742), mint green (993), rose (309), pink (776), orange (351), dark brown (898), and charcoal (413)
Graph paper; tapestry needle
Water-erasable pen

INSTRUCTIONS
Before beginning, see the general information on pages 78 and 79 for special cross-stitch tips and techniques.

Refer to the chart, *opposite,* for the sampler pattern. Chart the desired name, date, and weight onto graph paper, using the chart as a guide. Use the alphabet in the design or refer to other alphabets in the book.

Measure 3 inches down and 3 inches in from the upper left corner of the fabric; mark this point with a water-erasable pen. Begin stitching there.

Use two strands of floss to work cross-stitches and backstitches over one square of the fabric. Work cross-stitches first, then work backstitches, French knots, and straight stitches as follow:

Use two strands of dark brown floss to work the backstitches to outline the teddy bears. Use one strand of dark brown floss to work butterfly antennae.

Use two strands of the charcoal floss to work French knots for bears' noses and ducks' eyes, and to backstitch baby's weight. Use one strand of charcoal to backstitch the bear grins and balloon strings. With two strands of the orange floss, embroider straight stitches for duck beaks.

Frame as desired.

Cross-Stitch Doll

Shown on pages 60–61.

Finished doll is 21½ inches tall.

MATERIALS
For the doll
15x36-inch piece of white hardanger
DMC embroidery floss in the following colors: scraps of rose (603), light pink (776), dark gray (413), yellow (727), purple (209), and green (562); 1 skein *each* of blue (793), dark brown (975), light brown (976), gold (977), lavender (211), aqua (519), and dark pink (956)
1 yard of ½-inch-wide pregathered eyelet
14 inches of 2-inch-wide pregathered eyelet
1 yard of ¼-inch-wide pink satin ribbon
2 small buttons for shoe straps
Polyester fiberfill

For the dress and bonnet
¾ yard of 45-inch-wide printed cotton fabric
¾ yard of narrow lace
⅓ yard of narrow elastic
3 small snaps
25-inch strip of 1½-inch-wide white cotton
Scrap of fusible interfacing

For the pinafore
18x40-inch piece of white hardanger
DMC embroidery floss in the following colors: dark blue (517), light blue (518), dark green (562), light green (563), dark purple (209), light purple (211), dark pink (335), and light pink (776)
1 yard of narrow picot lace trim
1 yard of 1-inch-wide satin white ribbon
10x12-inch scrap of white lining fabric
12-inch length of ⅜-inch-wide white grosgrain ribbon

INSTRUCTIONS
For the doll
Note: All pattern pieces include ¼-inch seam allowances, except the neck edge of the head and body, which includes a ¾-inch seam allowance.

Enlarge patterns, page 72, and use a water-erasable pen to trace each doll body piece onto the hardanger. (Make sure patterns lie on the straight grain of the fabric.) Do not cut until cross-stitching is complete.

Referring to charts, pages 73 and 74, work each cross-stitch over one thread of hardanger, using one strand of floss. Locate center of each design and center of each fabric piece and begin cross-stitching there.

Work the cross-stitches on the *front* of head only. Work one body piece in cross-stitches for the undergarment. Then stitch the vertical striping on the undergarment with purple using backstitches over two threads of the fabric.

Stitch the right shoe on one leg piece; then work the mirror image on second leg for left shoe. Stitch the backs of shoes on remaining two leg pieces, eliminating the flower motif and the buckle strap.

When stitching is complete, cut out shapes along the outside of the drawn lines and machine-stitch around the tracing lines.

With right sides facing, sew the body pieces together, leaving the neck open. Clip, turn, and stuff. Repeat for head. Sew head to the body, adding more of the stuffing as needed to keep neck firm.

With right sides facing, sew arms together in pairs, leaving tops open. Clip, turn, and stuff. Turn tops in and sew to body. Repeat for legs.

Referring to the photo, page 61, hand-sew one strip of ½-inch eyelet along dotted line of *upper* body. Sew one strip of the ½-inch eyelet atop the 2-inch eyelet strip; then hand-sew this strip along dotted line of *lower* body. Hand-sew remaining strip of eyelet slightly above the strip just sewn to lower body. Finish all ends at center back.

continued

FANCIFUL TREASURES

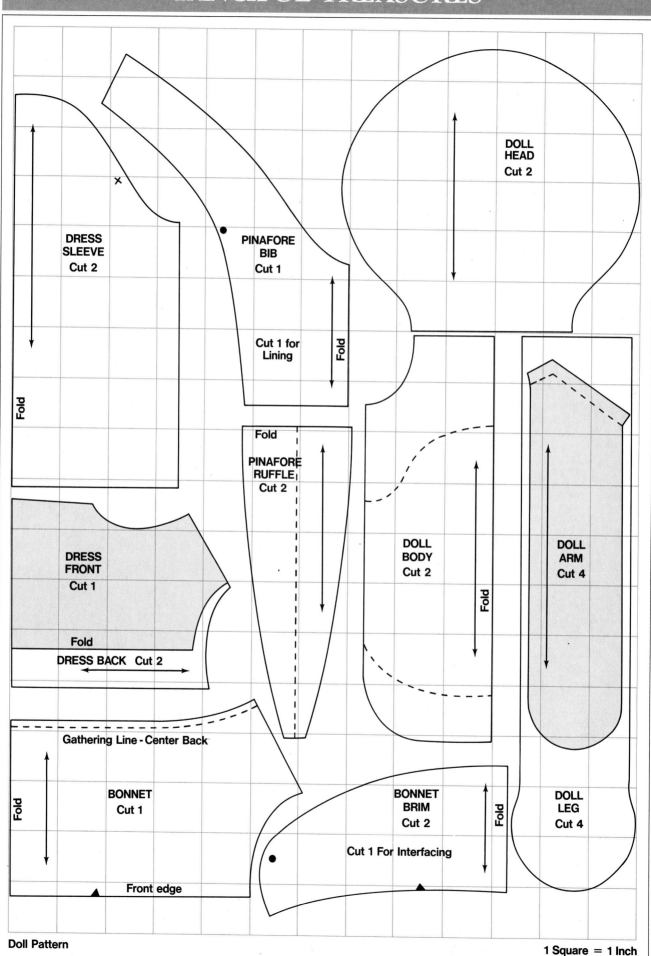

DRESS
SLEEVE
Cut 2

Fold

×

PINAFORE
BIB
Cut 1

Cut 1 for
Lining

Fold

DOLL
HEAD
Cut 2

Fold

PINAFORE
RUFFLE
Cut 2

DRESS
FRONT
Cut 1

Fold

DRESS BACK Cut 2

DOLL
BODY
Cut 2

Fold

DOLL
ARM
Cut 4

Gathering Line - Center Back

Fold

BONNET
Cut 1

BONNET
BRIM
Cut 2

Cut 1 For Interfacing

Fold

DOLL
LEG
Cut 4

Front edge

Doll Pattern

1 Square = 1 Inch

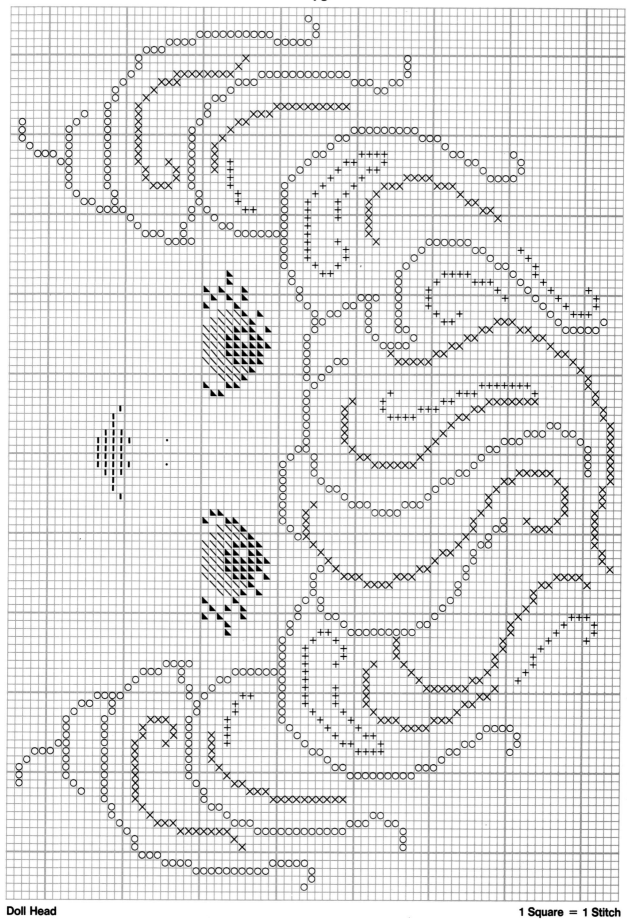

Doll Head

1 Square = 1 Stitch

COLOR KEY

975	⊙ Brown	977	⊞ Golden Brown	603	⊟ Rose	413	◪ Dark Gray
976	⊠ Light Brown	793	◨ Blue	776	◉ Light Pink		

FANCIFUL TREASURES

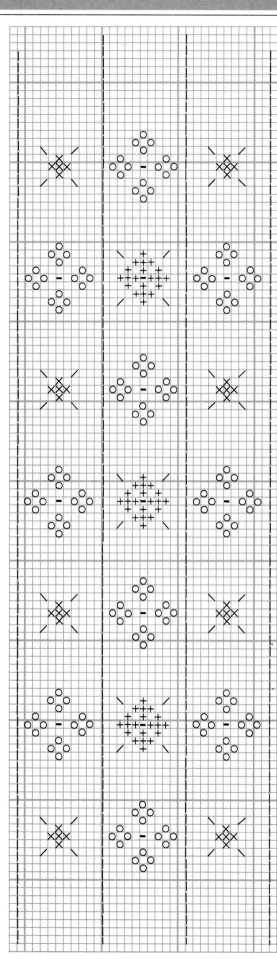

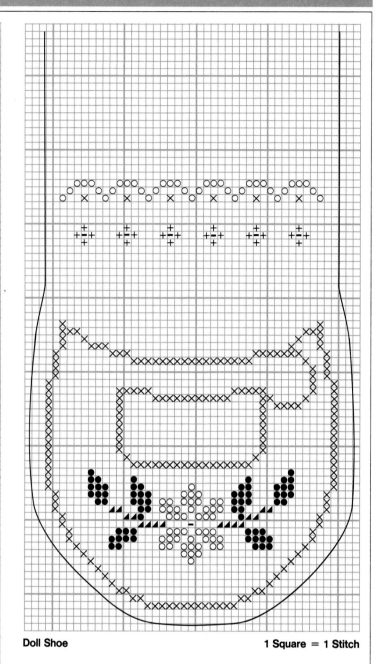

Doll Shoe

1 Square = 1 Stitch

COLOR KEY

519	⊠	Aqua
956	⊙	Dark Pink
211	⊞	Light Purple
727	⊟	Yellow
562	◪	Dark Green
563	●	Light Green

Backstitch Colors

☐ Dark Purple

☐ Dark Green

☐ Dark Green

Doll Undergarment

1 Square = 1 Stitch

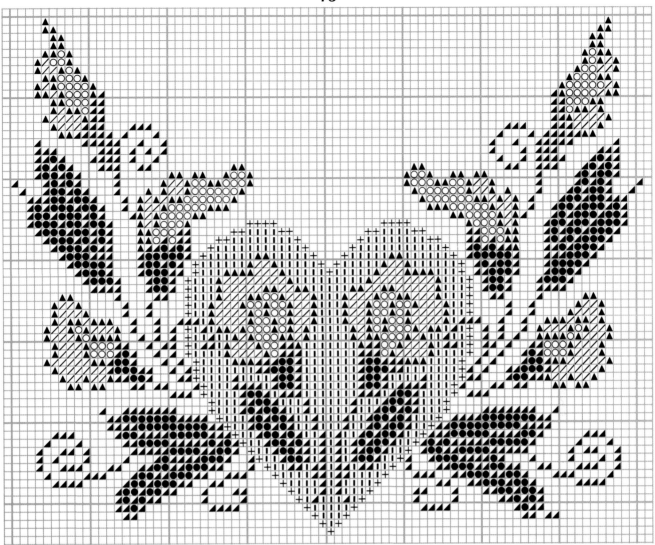

Pinafore Bib 1 Square = 1 Stitch

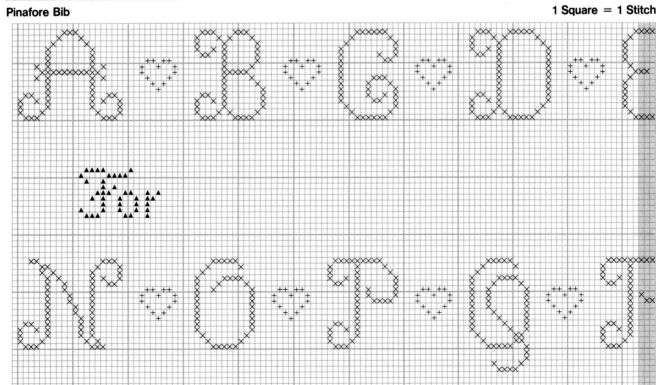

Pinafore - Left Skirt 1 Square = 1 Stitch

COLOR KEY 517 ⊠ Dark Blue 562 ◪ Dark Green 209 ▲ Dark Purple 335 ⊞ Dark Pink

518 ◪ Light Blue 563 ● Light Green 211 ○ Light Purple 776 ⊡ Light Pink

FANCIFUL TREASURES

Cut the ribbon into four equal lengths; tie into bows. Sew three to torso to complete the undergarment. Sew buttons to shoe straps.

For the dress

Cut the dress front, backs, and sleeves from fabric as directed. For skirt, cut piece measuring 11½x38 inches.

With right sides facing, sew front to backs at shoulders. Staystitch along neck edge.

To make center back facings, fold back ½ inch of center back edges, right sides facing, and sew along neck edge only. Turn facing and neck edge to inside; press. With right sides facing, sew lace along neck edge; turn lace under at center backs. Clip along neckline edge; fold lace edging up.

Run two rows of gathering stitches between the two Xs on the sleeves. With right sides facing, pin, then sew, sleeves to armholes, gathering to fit. For casing, press, then sew, ¼ inch of sleeve bottoms twice. Sew lace along sleeve bottom edges. Insert elastic and pull up to fit wrist of doll. Sew across both ends. Sew bodice and sleeve underarm seams.

Run gathering stitches along one long edge of skirt. Pin to bodice, pulling up gathers to fit; sew. Sew a ½-inch center back seam for 7 inches from bottom of skirt. Press under ¼ inch at bottom of skirt; then press under 1 inch for hem; hand-sew hem. Sew snaps, evenly spaced, to bodice back.

For the bonnet

Cut bonnet and brim pieces from fabric as directed. Cut a bias strip 1¼x30 inches, piecing as necessary for bonnet ties.

Fold white strip in half, raw edges even, and gather to fit bonnet front edge. With right sides facing, sew in place.

Fuse interfacing to wrong side of one brim piece; sew this piece to bonnet front edge, matching notches. With right sides facing, sew remaining brim piece to the interfaced piece; sew between circles only. Clip seams, turn, and press. Sew brim through all thicknesses to bonnet front edge.

Run gathering stitches along the gathering lines of bonnet and gather tightly; then tie and secure gathering threads. Sew the center back seam, right sides facing,

Fold, then press under ¼ inch on both the long raw edges of the bias strip. Fold the strip in half, having folded lines even.

Locate the center of the bias strip and center back of bonnet; pin, then sew lower edges of bonnet to bias strip. Sew folded bias strip on both sides of bonnet together. Tie knots in both ends of ties. Sew remaining ribbon bow to center back over gathering.

For the pinafore

Use a water-erasable pen and draw a rectangle measuring 9x12 inches onto the hardanger for bib. For skirt, draw a rectangle measuring 9½x20 inches. Make sure shapes lie on the straight grain of the fabric. Do not cut pieces from fabric until crossstitching is complete.

BIB: Refer to chart at top of page 75 and begin stitching the design in the center of the fabric, ¾ inch from the bottom edge, working the cross-stitches over one thread of the fabric with one strand of floss. The stitch at the tip of the heart is the first stitch. Work the complete design.

Pinafore - Center Skirt

1 Square = 1 Stitch

COLOR KEY							
517 ⊠ Dark Blue	562 ◪ Dark Green	209 ▲ Dark Purple	335 ⊞ Dark Pink
518 ⊘ Light Blue	563 ● Light Green	211 ○ Light Purple	776 ⊡ Light Pink

SKIRT: Locate the center of the fabric crosswise and mark with a water-erasable pen. The heart motif on the chart on page 76 is the center of the skirt design; begin stitching from this chart, 2½ inches from the edge of the fabric. Begin with the stitch at the bottom of the heart.

Complete this chart and then work from the charts on pages 75 and 77 to complete the design along the bottom of the skirt. *Note:* The shaded portions of the charts represent stitches already completed from the chart on page 76. Do not work the shaded areas.

When all stitching is complete, cut out shapes along the outside of the drawn lines, the bib ruffle, and a strip of fabric 1x8½ inches for the waistband. Machine-stitch around all cut pieces. Cut bib piece from lining fabric.

ASSEMBLY: Fold ruffles in half lengthwise and gather along raw edges to fit between small circles on bib. With right sides facing, sew ruffles to bib. Sew the lace around neckline and bib straps, right sides facing. Sew facing to bib piece, right sides together, leaving bottom of bodice and ends of straps open. Clip seams, turn, and press.

Sew lace ½ inch from bottom of skirt edge; then turn under ½-inch hem so lace runs along bottom edge of skirt and hand-sew hem in place.

Turn under ¼ inch on both sides of skirt and machine-sew. Repeat again to finish side edges.

Run gathering threads along top edge of skirt; gather up to 8 inches. Match center front of waistband to center front of skirt. With right sides together, sew waistband to skirt, leaving ¼-inch allowance on both the short ends of the waistband.

With right sides together, sew bodice to top of band, matching center fronts, and sew ends of shoulder straps ¼ inch from center back. Sew ribbon ties to waistband, pleating to fit.

To finish waistband, sew grosgrain ribbon along top half of wrong side of waistband. Slipstitch ribbon over the seam allowance at bottom edge of waistband, tucking in ends of skirt, ends of ribbon ties, and ¼-inch waistband edges.

Child's Pinafore

Shown on page 61.

MATERIALS
Commercial pinafore pattern
White cotton fabric (yardage as specified in pattern)
10-count waste canvas: 1 11x40-inch piece for skirt; 1 10x12-inch piece for bib; and 1 6x8-inch piece for pockets
DMC floss in the colors cited for Doll Pinafore, page 71

INSTRUCTIONS
Trace the pattern pieces onto the fabric. Chart the child's name in place on chart, page 75.

Center and baste the waste canvas atop the traced fabric pieces. Allow the canvas to extend 2 inches beyond the stitching designs on all pieces.

Refer to Pinafore instructions, *opposite,* for working the cross-stitches, *except* use three threads of floss to work over one space of the canvas.

Remove the waste canvas and assemble pinafore following pattern instructions.

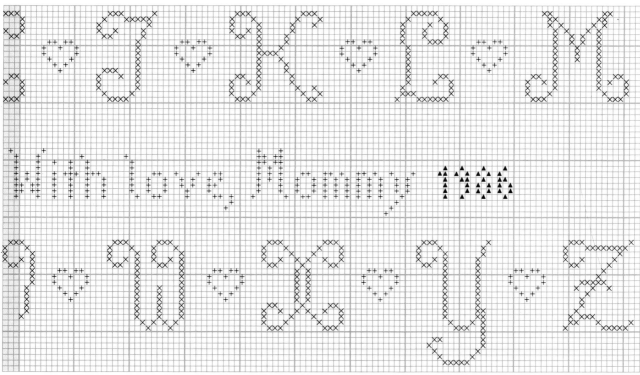

Pinafore - Right Skirt

1 Square = 1 Stitch

TIPS AND TECHNIQUES

Counted cross-stitch is a delightful craft, and one that's easy to master. Learn just one basic stitch, and the technique is at your fingertips!

To guide you through the sampler projects in this book, here are tips for selecting patterns, threads, fabrics, and needles, as well as finishing and blocking techniques.

Start with a Pattern

Assemble pattern materials

Many of the designs in this book can be stitched directly from the charts. For some designs, however, we've included only a portion of the pattern (one half or one fourth, for example). These need to be charted onto graph paper so you have a complete chart to stitch from.

Before you begin, assemble the following materials and supplies: masking tape, graph paper, felt-tip marking pens or colored pencils, a ruler, pencils, mat knife, and scissors.

GRAPH PAPER: Graph paper comes in many grid sizes, such as 4, 10, and 14 squares to the inch. Because the grids in this book are marked in increments of 10, graph paper with 10 squares per inch is probably the easiest to use for charting.

Graph paper pads and sheets come in a variety of sizes as well. Select the size that best accommodates your design. If you have to piece sheets, carefully align the squares, then tape them together on the *reverse* side.

COLORED PENCILS AND PENS: Gather pencils or felt-tip pens in shades that correspond to those on the color key for the pattern you intend to stitch.

Working from a chart

Before beginning to stitch, it is important to start with a complete and accurate pattern. Cross-stitch patterns are charted on grids with special symbols that represent the colors of thread used for embroidery. Symbols are noted in the color key and accompany each pattern.

Look carefully at the pattern given in the book and locate the center of the *finished* design. Next find the center of the graph paper. With a ruler and a pencil, draw horizontal and vertical lines on the graph paper, marking the center of the height and the center of the width, respectively.

Starting from this point, begin marking crosses with colored pens or pencils. Chart the diagram as it appears in the book, then flop the pattern, making one or more mirror images of the printed chart on your graph paper pattern.

If you make a mistake when charting the pattern, simply eliminate the mistake, using white typewriter correction fluid. If the error is over a large area, cut out the mistake with a mat knife and patch the hole with additional graph paper taped to the wrong side of the pattern.

Choose Materials

Even-weave fabrics

You can work counted cross-stitches on many fabrics. Even-weave fabrics are the obvious choice, but by using waste canvas, cross-stitches can be worked on many closely woven fabrics.

In even-weave fabrics, the vertical and horizontal threads are the same thickness throughout the cloth. Fabrics come in many colors and thread counts, allowing great flexibility in the size of the finished design.

HARDANGER CLOTH: This is one of the more common fabrics used for counted thread work. The thread count is *always* 22 threads per inch.

AIDA CLOTH: This cloth appears to be made of tiny squares and is an excellent choice for beginners because the squares define the area for working each stitch. Aida cloth comes in many sizes—6-, 8-, 11-, 14-, and 18-count.

MONO NEEDLEPOINT CANVAS: Experiment with cross-stitches on mono needlepoint canvas, leaving the background unworked. It, too, is available in a variety of thread counts.

WASTE CANVAS: Waste canvas is a special even-weave material that allows you to work counted cross-stitches atop fabrics other than even-weaves.

Stitches worked over waste-canvas look exactly like stitches worked on even-weave fabric. But waste canvas enables you to embroider on batiste, cotton, broadcloth, gabardine, poplin, wool, and many other tightly woven fabrics.

This canvas is available in sizes ranging from 6 to 16 squares per linear inch. The canvas can be pieced, but it is preferable to purchase an amount that covers the entire area to be stitched.

Lay canvas atop fabric, making sure the grid of the canvas is even with the grain of the fabric. Pin and baste the canvas in place.

To work the stitches, insert the threaded needle into the *smallest* squares of the canvas. Be careful not to catch the canvas when stitching; otherwise, removing the canvas threads will be difficult and stitches will be pulled out of shape.

When the stitching is complete, moisten canvas; pull out the horizontal threads, one at a time and in order. Then, pull the vertical threads until the canvas is completely removed.

Yarns and Threads

Select threads

The colors and variety of thread and yarn choices are enormous. Here are some of the more traditional materials used for cross-stitch projects.

EMBROIDERY FLOSS: Six-strand floss is available in the widest range of colors of any thread. Flosses are available in 100 percent cotton, rayon, or silk. Whether you use one, two, or all six strands for stitching depends upon the fabric and number of threads each stitch is worked over.

PEARL COTTON: Pearl cotton is available in three sizes—Nos. 3, 5, and 8. (No. 3 is thick; No. 8 is thin.) This floss has an obvious twist and a high sheen.

WOOL YARN: A single strand of three-ply wool gives a rich look to cross-stitches. Wool yarns work best on loosely woven fabrics.

Working with threads

Cut thread into lengths that you find comfortable to work with (18 inches is a good length). However, cut unusual threads that fray easily—rayons, silks, or metallics—into shorter lengths for finer looking stitching. Knot the cut strands loosely together, and mark them with the appropriate color number.

Types of Needles

Distinguishing needle styles

Needles come in all shapes and sizes; they may be thick or thin, wide- or narrow-eyed, long or short, and sharp- or blunt-pointed. The needle you select depends upon the threads and fabrics used for your project.

TAPESTRY NEEDLES: Tapestry needles have long eyes for holding multiple plies of thread, but the end of the needle is blunt rather than sharp. Use these needles to stitch on mono needlepoint canvas, perforated paper, and even-weave fabrics because they will not catch or snag the materials.

EMBROIDERY NEEDLES: Also called crewel needles, embroidery needles have the long eye characteristic of tapestry needles, but also have a sharp point for stitching on closely woven fabrics. Embroidery needles are ideal when you are working with embroidery flosses, Nos. 5 or 8 pearl cotton, metallic threads, or one ply of three-ply wool yarn.

CHENILLE NEEDLES: Chenille needles have the same qualities as embroidery needles, but they are available only in a larger range of sizes. Longer eyes make them ideal for crewel embroidery and for stitching with wool yarn or No. 8 pearl cotton.

Stitching the Design

Select a starting point

The point at which you begin to stitch varies with each design. Usually the center of the pattern is best, but beginning in a corner is appropriate if you are certain of the finished size of your project.

Allow extra fabric around the design for framing. You may wish to leave a border of plain fabric around the stitchery *before* framing, and you must allow excess fabric for stretching the stitchery around the backing material.

Using masking tape, bind edges of the fabric to prevent raveling.

Beginning and ending a stitch

The best way to begin a cross-stitch is by using a *waste knot*. It is a temporary knot and will be clipped later. To begin, knot the end of a threaded needle. Insert the needle into the right side of the fabric, about 4 inches away from placement of the first cross-stitch. Bring the needle up through the fabric and work the first series of cross-stitches. Stitch until the thread is used up or until the area to be filled with this color is complete.

To finish the thread, slip the threaded needle under the previously stitched threads on the wrong side of the fabric for 1 to 1½ inches. (You may wish to weave the thread back and forth a few times.) Clip the thread.

Turn the piece to the right side and clip the waste knot. Rethread the needle with the excess floss and push the needle to the wrong side of the stitchery. Fasten the thread as directed above.

Working a cross-stitch

A finished cross-stitch is square. The number of threads of fabric that a cross-stitch is worked over varies from project to project. (See project instructions.) The important points to remember are to make stitches a uniform size, and to *work all topstitches in the same direction.*

To make a cross-stitch, pull the threaded needle from the wrong side of the fabric through the appropriate hole in the even-weave fabric. Carry the needle across and up the appropriate number of threads and insert it in the upper right corner of the square the stitch will fill.

The second part of the stitch begins in the lower right corner of the square. Bring the needle up through the fabric and carry it across the required number of threads, inserting it into the fabric at the upper left corner of the square, finishing the stitch.

Maintain uniform stitches

When embroidering, always keep stitch tension uniform. If threads are pulled too taut, the fabric and stitches become distorted. If threads are too loose, the shape of the stitches is lost.

Carrying threads

When working with areas that use a variety of thread colors, you need not end your thread every time you use a color. Carry the thread across the back of the fabric, but, to secure the thread, slip the threaded needle under previously stitched crosses. If you carry the threads *loosely* to another area, without securing the thread, the piece can easily become distorted.

Blocking the stitchery

Once you have completed the stitchery, remove the tape from the raw edges. Lay a thick cloth over your ironing board and place the stitchery right side down over the cloth. Dampen a pressing cloth and lay it atop the stitchery. Then press the piece using a moderately hot iron.

After blocking, the embroidery is ready for you to frame or assemble into your project.

ACKNOWLEDGMENTS

Our special thanks to the following designers who contributed projects to this book. When more than one project appears on a page, the acknowledgment specifically cites the project with the page number. A page number alone indicates one designer or source has contributed all of the project material listed for that page.

Taresia Boernke—60–61
Laura Holtorf Collins—7; 9, adaptation from fire screen on page 8; 10 and 12, adaptations from sampler on page 11; 32–33, adaptations from flower sampler on pages 30–31; 54–55, adaptations from teddy bear sampler on pages 52–53; 56–57
Dixie Falls—4–5
Diane Hayes—11; 30–31; 36; 52–53; 59
Jane Kennelly—13
Beverly Rivers—8; 58, lamb pillow toy
Margaret Sindelar—60–61, doll apron and bonnet
Patricia Sparks—34–35; 58, birth bear toy
Jim Williams—37
Dee Wittmack—6

We also are pleased to acknowledge the following photographers, whose talents and technical skills contributed much to this book.

Mike Dieter—4–5; 6–7; 8; 10; 13;
Hopkins Associates—30–31; 32–33; 35; 36; 52–53; 54–55; 56–57; 58; 60–61
William Hopkins—34; 37
Jim Kascoutas—9; 11; 12
Scott Little—59

For their creative skills, courtesy, and cooperation, we extend a special thanks to:

Lu Ann Bagnall
Barbara Bergman
Gary Boling
Patricia Bradshaw
Germaine Eagleton
Jackie Fees
Donna Glas
Nancy Helgeson
Sara Donna Jenson
Diane Pratt
Jil Severson
Julie Whitney
Julie Wiemann

For their cooperation and courtesy, we extend a special thanks to the following sources:

Astor Place, Ltd.
239 Main Ave.
Stirling, NJ 07980
C.M. Offray & Son, Inc.
261 Madison Ave.
New York, NY 10016
DMC Corporation
197 Trumbull St.
Elizabeth, NJ 07206
Gutcheon Patchworks, Inc.
611 Broadway
New York, NY 10012
Joan Toggit Ltd.
246 Fifth Ave.
New York, NY 10001
The Tyke Corporation
1165 N. Clark St.
Suite 400
Chicago, IL 60610

Pella Historical Society
Pella, Iowa